SCUM

Scum

Paul Williams

KARNAC

First published in 2013 by
Karnac Books Ltd
118 Finchley Road
London NW3 5HT

British Library Cataloguing in Publication Data

A C.I.P. for this book is available from the British Library

ISBN-13: 978-1-78049-174-5

Typeset by V Publishing Solutions Pvt Ltd., Chennai, India

www.karnacbooks.com

Scum:
a film or layer of foul or extraneous matter
refuse or offscourings
a low, worthless, or evil person
riffraff, dregs

Adolescence is a difficult time. Adolescence without a childhood that precedes it is an incomprehensible time. As children grow, experiences multiply, facts proliferate, and minds are needed to think and to help. An adolescent without a mind, without another mind to help, is like a steel ball that ricochets around a pinball machine without stopping. Thinking founders, language does not stick, emotion becomes an arch enemy. How do you write about such things when language—words, talking, writing—has failed? To at least try is the purpose of this book, which addresses breakdown and some of its consequences, including for language.

Paul Williams
Hampshire, UK
2012

vii

Also by the author
The Fifth Principle

To Kenneth McMorine

*I am grateful to Alice Jones, Catherine McKenzie,
Thomas Ogden, Eric Rhode, and Annie Sweetnam for
their valuable comments on this manuscript*

CONTENTS

CHAPTER ONE

Onward and upward

Summer came went as it does what was left of it spent in The Woods no longer alone boys turned up some to play others to shoot sparrows blue tits heat frogs in milk bottles until they swelled up and burst scanned them all talked to no-one hid in bushes avoid the ones who killed the animals   protest   against cruelty   rose in his throat finding no voice turned away feelings quashed. Hated a small refined cat the woman called mother bought dismissed it tormented frightened it it hated back didn't feel like a sick dance he did to it what she did to him what boys did to animals   what he   did   to   himself.

Birthday eleven unnoticed grammar school signalled the end of The Woods eight years refuge no sadness dampness settled into him as if left out in the rain though the summer sun still shone couldn't move didn't want to sit for long periods cast down less vigilant not noticing not caring. A ghost can prevent detection but the energy to keep the security camera running ran out paid the price.

"Gerrout yer fuckin' l'il wanker."

Animal killers kicked beat drove him out of The Woods requiring he check before entering   something   not done   before   retraced at dawn trails hideouts before the summer melted the main pond the fallen log dugout Europe South America darkest Asia China bulrush pond ditch imprinted branded on his body if he could pacing back forth touch each in turn. The most intense memories save the violence are of The Woods colours textures smells heat cold sunshine stillness dignity of ancient trees alive in him today groups of tall peaceful adults not complaining of comings and goings creaking their familiar welcome standing by him whispering contentment with any game, any time, including when tired eyes closed their rustling goodbye never harsh a reminder they would be there waiting. Things went wrong in The Woods but not enough to destroy the tie not even at the final goodbye he had to leave   they   knew.

Years later in the area for the aftermath fear the house where it had happened nothing. Familiar no feature marker of the past small grey box mass of small grey boxes drab grey street at one point glanced at the window upstairs bare bedroom he'd slept quiver down back cold feeling moved on. Seeing The Woods altogether different   they   had   vanished   submerged beneath a sea of cheap houses as far as the eye could see The Woods pond cornfield swept away smeared with packing cases strewn either side of pinched liquorice streets writhing nowhere body blow.

"Vandals ... vandals!"

Shouted silently dumbstruck heaving goulash of rubble palmed off as improvement belief beggared row upon row of hutches spattered like shit from a dung spreader in the name of prosperity home ownership for all identical houses cars people shrunk handkerchief gardens you couldn't swing a cat nothing alive maybe indoors like the grey box. Shock anger gave way to grief salvage something a mental ordnance survey map no landmark hill undulation woods tree remained everything uprooted flattened give up in disgust keep The Woods alive inside if nowhere else.

Autumn came went as it does old double decker bus from the corner of the street to the grammar school packed rowdy children eleven to eighteen a few sitting silently followed their example recognised no-one.

"Worra you lookin' a' new boy, eh?"
"Nothing."
"Ope so, gobshite."

The air of a pariah beaten-down children are quick to spot. No seat safe.

"Eh! New boy. Gizz ya dinner money."
"No. I haven't got any."
"You want yer bag to go out da window, den? Gizz yer fuckin' money, shit face."
"Haven't got any."
"Wha'?! Show us yer pockets, yer lyin' bastard."
"See?"
"Pathetic l'il fucker. When yer get money, we wann it. Gorrit, creep?"

3

Stand next to the conductor safe the exit fresh air rushing scene calmed him made him more not less conspicuous taking the bus an ordeal often skipped in favour of walking the streets. The idea of retaliating against bullying did not occur then nor during six years of grammar school the fact of gangs terror like the woman called mother's random attacks one trait made them deadly never knowing when where the next would come from. Surprise artefact a different logic uncanny sixth sense for when he was off-guard calmer consoled elsewhere away from her the grey box triggered the least expected explosion for no reason a hail of abuse everything upside down whatever was experienced wasn't never had been. Thought he expected it thinking himself ready for it   wasn't   shell-shocked hoped for end invited end implored end from the age of three four as little to do with her violence rejected laudable no doubt unbeknown to him feelings of injustice fury disconnect such that when bullied each battering unprecedented happened for the first time it wasn't it was. To retaliate an impossible blunder to be avoided at any cost like dying exception one protest only ever forced change he did not plan could not have foreseen. The man called father not the woman called mother not the school bullies after starting grammar school the man's derision seeped deep in him mocked dismissed anything said done melodramatic hot air empty boasting puffed-up exhibitionist mummy's boy. Cleaning shoes mud washed off old tin polish spread the man called father seized them with the assurance of an expert sat back in his chair here's how it is done.

> *"You don't know how to do this! I've been doin' it for years. Let me show you how it's done properly … give 'em 'ere."*

Asked for shoes back ignored performance underway the man called father drunk? Unaccountably trying to help? Asked again swatted away one too many humiliating taunts of uselessness.

> *"Watch and learn, sunshine. Kids don't know anything … and mummy's boys definitely don't."*

Rage lava boiled head toe drew back fist exploded   one punch   on the jaw   ***"Fuck Off!"***   man chair flew backwards dazed wide-eyed speechless floor chin corner of mouth announced with preposterous formality.

> *"I never expected to hear such foul language in THIS house."*

The child called son's turn to be speechless guilt halted in its tracks even the woman called mother in the door to catch the action lost for words a first? The man filled the house with foul language every day for as long as anyone remembered how could holier-than-thou double standards like these be lost on him? "Fuck off" foul language after day after day after month after month after year after year.

> *"Bastard" "hewer" "tart" "filth", "cow" "idiot" "windbag" "retard."*

Self-righteousness might have been funny smashing cant from a vain coward brought no pleasure a vague feeling of doing the right thing never understood until years later why the man's derision stopped from that moment never to return.

Getting off the bus a relief on the first day of grammar school what lay ahead wasn't an enormous stone building biggest in the world stretched for miles hordes of insect children in black jacket casings swarmed through doorways a trail down a wood-lined corridor into a quadrangle crammed with insects running shouting shoving anxiety fear dread no escape the commotion penned him in a packed courtyard anything could happen any moment no capacity to resist after the bus bullying body mind in pieces nothing new recourse stillness hid behind corner pillar back against cold concrete eyes shut nothing. Seemed hours probably minutes a whistle blast cut the racket old bald wiry man black gown ordered insects into lines smallest tallest to the back of smallest line head down one eye on tall insects filed into large wood glass doors hundreds of insects seething row upon row of wood chairs flanked by teachers in black gowns   crows and insects   on a far stage crow squawking clung to seat convinced the wrong one head down invisible took in nothing agonised over shoelace undone not undone surely seen by a crow   worm   for   a   crow reached to check signal to get him don't do it. What if the wormlace were seen? Punished thrown out worse? Was this a *wish?* He was the black spot untouchable wrong everything should never have been there *was* a wish to be anywhere else here was a truth that takes a lifetime to unearth.

Infestation of hall ended the way it began trailing insects poured into the quadrangle again supervising staring stalking crows latched onto a small colony tried to conceal wormlace under other foot corralled into "houses" a "house" the colour of your tie clusters of ties marched off to classroom blur escalating confusion desks registration books lessons timetables on top of the crow commotion splintered disarray what passed for a mind snapped to attention snapped snapped again ricocheted around the room appearing to be in attendance eyes rattled burnt out ached motionless.

Within days rat pack of bullies some from his class some from the class above identified fresh quarry lumbering numbskull leader Malcolm Hanton moose-like bellowed brayed spat toothy menace to wrench submission from prey.

> *"'Allo, li'l fucker, wos dis den?"*
> *"Wos yer name, arsehole?"*
> *"Cum on yer fuckin' shitbag, say it den or you know wha'."*

Rats joined the chant pinned the victim in a corner at which point Hanton loses interest a gambit scratched moose brain knee him crying fresh wheeze.

> *"Worrabout dis den shitbag … Wibbler, fuckin' Wibbler!"*

Inspired a further variation

> *"WibblAAAH, WibblAAAH fuckin' li'l PiddlAAAH."*

Bullying six years no one intervened even in full view of teachers hid in copse wasn't missed small wood on the edge of school playing field relieved at first smaller than The Woods less protection. What had happened to him? Where were The Woods?

Brawn no brain Hanton's scheming toadying hitman Iago reptile Smith took advantage of prey when the moose had his fill of a pale neglected wisp of a boy called Riley albino eyes the reptile's favourite reacted ghost-like spoke to no one couldn't be hurt already killed. He is

7

ashamed he looked down on Riley to make himself feel superior smelly stupid rotten unwanted avoid contamination today the similarity of their circumstances only too obvious. Riley didn't run from warped attackers the way he did but confronted them with the defiance of the damned no rise bad sport turned their attention to a new target fresh with panic great entertainment no fight back fight back made him into her impossible never her they were her not him. Did not know under attack he felt noticed better than a lifetime of indifference retaliation suicidal avoid threats obvious isn't it except it isn't obvious you can't avoid everything especially when you don't know you don't want to avoid everything. Moose toad took him "by surprise" he "forgot" to go to school do classwork homework steered clear *others* are hostile not him as an adult wondered whether this is what psychiatrists call paranoia perhaps it is and he was and is paranoid. Attacks from twelve months until leaving the greyboxschoolcountry at seventeen terrified him take this this THIS and THIS!   "get off"   "leave me alone"   couldn't say didn't say why not? The mother father attacked him not he them surely it was this way round wasn't it? It was wasn't it? Shame isolation meant he thought it wasn't it was him recoiled from himself not trusting anyone terrified of attacks whose attacks theirs his? His. Theirs. Terrified of terror can you imagine? Dread of her expert timing over and over again dying not once twice repeatedly attackers powerful surely it was this way round wasn't it? Sooner not later attacks came no matter what disgrace inside outside no hope consolation despair save life limb self-slaughter as only the timing of the final moment left no consorting with people stay alive have the story verified by a reliable witness over time who comes within spitting distance of this? Who says witness is reliable?

Two grammar school events changed him one unbeknown for the worse one unbeknown for the better fell in love with Mr Carragher geography teacher complicated love how he looked young fit Welshman from the valleys thick accent army officer authority clean upstanding serious-minded tweed jacket leather patches grey flannel picture of integrity not like the man called father anyone else. Carragher didn't tolerate indiscipline growling barking prize-winning dog penning in sheep astonished by Carragher's controlled temper (not having one himself) smouldering volcano snarled thundered roared rugby floodplains Carboniferous Period ammonites eyes blazed listening not to him to the sound of his voice picked up punished impress him memorise lessons top marks in geography without understanding a word Carragher pleased he over the moon. Took an interest in all things Welsh including his own name stories of miners from South Wales underground coal formations made of petrified forests male voice choirs sing to express solidarity   "solidarity"   a great word went to a Birkenhead record shop listening booth heard a male voice choir transported didn't last lessons more and more complicated grey box worse if such a thing could be attacks brawls no place to do homework grammar school bullies grey box hamstrung mess after mess demolished what was left the end a matter of time.

Hanton toad nest of rats trapped him in a stairwell after school.

> *"Carragher's fuckin' bum boy, Carragher's fuckin' bum boy."*

People gone no one around last moment had come knew it   a   wish? Terror slid him into a ball head held.

> *"Stop it, please stop it. You have broken my jaw."*

Do you hear this? Wholesale disgrace demolition uncovered years later smashing the jaw of the man called father stop cruelty blamed shamed himself for the man called father's revenge you'd think standing up for himself would have given him courage wouldn't you? It didn't. Why not? Holding onto the man called father by having himself humiliated? To a   "family"?   To a pack of rats? Lying? Telling the truth? Both? Roaring jeering took whimpering for the white flag it was rats strolled off crowing pain from the beating no match for burningfleshshameofbegginglikeadog spared the death he knew he deserved. Nothing left. Scum. Terror of dying gone threw in the towel mark of a crushed louse leave school first chance.

Losing Carragher someone he thought he could respect hanging on to every word misread Carragher's character worthlessness seeded by parents spores attached everywhere absurd incident signalled the end of his dealings with Carragher boys went into lavatory smoke cigarettes stayed outside stray on the edge of the pack afraid of smoking the man called father killed smoking they wouldn't have included him anyway wouldn't have wanted to be Carragher caught them red-handed.

"To the headmaster's office IMMEDIATELY" he rapped stamping out fags trooped off one or two smirking.

> *"And you"* Carragher said looking at him.
> *"But sir ..."* he spluttered.
> *"To the headmaster's office. Double quick!"*

Propelled by the collar into line of suspects frogmarched down corridor looked up Carragher tower of rage unafraid of being taken to the headmaster no respect for school hadn't smoked a farce afraid of offending Carragher still always right. Outside headmaster's door taken in one by one thwack of bamboo on buttock moose defiant treated it as a lark untouchable above the authority of anyone toad copied moose found it hard to walk the rest miserable one tearful. Last one in Carragher alongside caught smoking in the toilets deputy headmaster Oscar Wilson BSc (tall bald wiry crow in the quadrangle the first day) other side cane stiff against leg like a rifle. Headmaster, Mr B.H.T. Taylor MSc leaned across his desk.

> *"What do you have to say for yourself? This is a poor show, isn't it?"*
> *"I didn't do it, sir. I wasn't smoking."*

Intake of Carragher breath Wilson tap tap.

> *"You will receive six strokes of the cane"* Taylor continued wearily*"sign here."*

Large book names boys punished offence category "smoking" guilty before he'd come in! signed Wilson brought a wood chair bend over pulled up jacket six lustful cracks hurt terribly fourth numb tearless left as normal a posture as possible scissors cut hair crew cut no more talking.

Seeing integrity in a man like Carragher repeated mistake several times in life to his cost until childhood faced with clear eyes deceiving himself good people somewhere if not the people called parents aren't so bad after all why not? Concoction fake goodness façade slapped over predators no blueprint until truth of what happened what happens thinkable before thinking are you left with magic? Fiction? How is it a child appreciated The Woods stirred by warm lit driving past cars? Are infants programmed to look for good things or see ducks as swans? After ratsstairwellbeatingCarraghersmokingfarce

11

something died did it really die could he have known if something did die or is it fiction about unthinkable things turned into a story as if a story is possible a story written about unthinkable things that not only cannot be written cannot be thought about being an afterthought? Is death of children a fiction dead children write nothing else to do never will have the truth unthinkable died long ago before any story could be written what kind of story is this? No story at all. If he could be honest with himself he might have written he did not exist had not existed as far as he knew. You might suggest an afterthought for a no story a quiet requiem or homage to help him see think of it as acting on his behalf if it helps. No story of death inflicted on a no mind no person no story. You might suggest insofar as he thought he had glimpsed a star in the sky a star that looked like a star in the sky was a star that died thousands of light years earlier its image only now visible in the sky does not exist stopped existing a long time ago. If he can see this think of it as acting on his behalf   you   on   his   be   half.   You will need to think about what cannot be thought about what kind of story of death this might not be. No story at all. No story no person no thought only afterthought radio wave trace element. What kind of thinking of no story of death is this? No thinking no thinking at all. What saying can be said? No saying. What telling told? No telling. You can help him see there are not one but two philosophical questions one is suicide the other is the question of how you go about living life after death. Think of it as acting on his behalf if it helps.

The second of the two events at grammar school the one that went better for him unbeknown took place at the time he began to fail with Carragher but before thepeoplecalledparentsratsCarragherWilsonTaylor finished him off. He invented the French language single handed.

CHAPTER TWO

Out cold

Eternities earlier than grammar school drowned by the ritual of primary school wandering grey streets respite in The Woods the lug of tired frame through rusted gates slumped under words rotas that buried him. The Woods seemed to change even before animal killers chased him out for good their acceptance indifference on long wet days when he hurt himself went numb with cold wet prickling bitingly icy stinging itching spoiling what would happen if things got worse.

Primary school should have been better than the grey box wasn't. Stuck from the start why people were there they him filed into a classroom why do   they   do this walking into a room together?

Words

"Where d'ya get that pencil?"
"Wanna come to my house afta?"
"Have y'seen my satchel?"
"We've gorra a new cat."

Why these words? How did they know when to talk stop talking know what to say next? Silence desk lids open—how? All this all day every day no hope of work exhausted by noon fending off a thousand orienting disorienting events once twice caught sight of why they were there a shaft of dust sunlight painted a stripe across the room everyone settled at desks ready to begin   he   a   part of   them   convulsed ribs knifed passed out stone still awake out cold stabbed dying flesh pounded dust dust to dust crushing machinery oblivious to the fact the job long since complete donkey work rampant parasite contraption evaded by dissolving melting if this fails become an alien. Might the crusher pause malfunction detect a misshapen boulder? Never. Flesh blood nerve endings no longer exposed anxiety pain renewed convulsions all efforts futile uncaring risks to avoid crusher force useless. Ebbed away to the extent that he no longer had a foothold on the planet not distress a catastrophe as these far reaches lie within moments of extinction numb blind to the emergency all emergencies long since taken care of coma gave way to naked terror body dismembered floating shrivelled parts feet first legs then arms torso finally face head what was left of his mind thrashing snatching chasing after extremities in the time left before the rest disappears lost for good. Anyone shot into the void at these speeds enough to rip limb from limb who lives to tell the tale spends life in mortal panic unaware that the only thing of importance is to remain unaware of the irruption that killed them.

> *"Who is the ink monitor for today? Once the ink has been given out, I want you to open your books at page forty-three and we will look at the life of Hannibal and his great journey and then write a story."*

The complexity of these statements defies belief   who impossibly confusing.

> *"Who is today's ink monitor?"*

Who   a person no idea of a person if they exist what for? Pouring ink a person pouring ink no possible meaning purpose bodies walked like his were   body-persons   why were there not other bodies ink pouring how does a   body-person   know to pour ink not another? Should he be one isn't should he know does not know about a body-person? To the brink of action a bodypersonpouringink checked for fear of humiliation unable to take a single step. pens ink exist he could see them writing what for the best to hope for was to draw images that looked like   writing   stars ticks for marks indistinguishable from the real thing as futile as writing itself.

> *"Children, open your books at Chapter Four, page forty-three. Hannibal and his journey. We'll read the story and then I want you to write your own story, your version of what you've heard."*

Children   chapter   story   write.

Why history ink writing? A question is out of the question. History book useless history doesn't happen pain fights all over again. Books writing to be   read   writing gets on pages book wrapped in cardboard stranger's name chains of people webs events nothing safe silent scream.

> *"Remember, it is important to practise your reading regularly."*

The more he read the less he understood words sentences no story no writing nothing anywhere drone in head beat of blood in ear throbbed louder Hannibal army animals journey body-persons tinnitus nothing.

> *"Now that we know who Hannibal was, can anyone tell me why it was that he went on his journey?"*

So on each day books lead weights writing infection reading burst head The Woods brush of air cool horizon siphon off thoughts one by one the thread connecting them snaps appearance of listening worked when teacher occupied most of the time. Lifeless days long weekends wandering streets found him staring vacantly through railings guarding the silent school waiting for an inkling sign of movement as to where he left himself.

Life-death cannot avoid   people   no engagement no pleasure curiosity a toehold for survival cheat death appear to be alive to the menace that proceeds by stealth cunning not brute force poised in the shaft of dust sunlight to throw into relief all he had lost with a single deep slash. Children who re-enter from the void without complete burn-up know loss in their bodies minds long since pulverised. You don't ask an injured fox how it feels to have been crushed under the wheels of a truck do you? Cracked limbs cloud eyes jaw-dripping blood bile asphalt tell the story. So it is with children crusher works on plastic unformed jellyfish mind muscle cramps incontinence night terrors asthma nervous spasms seizures sickness. Kindness relaxation a glimpse of beauty rouses a marauding hooligan's gobby onslaughts scalpel stab faint migraine infection   "accident"   sets priorities straight again derision self-loathing. Electrical activity from the once nascent jelly mind a flicker in a solidified mass more like a turnstile or slot machine electrical spasm from corpse's instinctive response to a shaft of dust sunlight pummelled knifed *don't you get the message?* The more a beached whale thrashes the worse it gets better to yield to the arms of eternal rest when the time comes scrape together a means to withstand their cold embrace. A creature sat sought food avoided cruelty passed for a pupil external world pockmarked wallpaper couldn't sidestep peel away stomached it loathed its rank fog drew him onto conveyor belts in unwanted directions. Body-persons appeared disappeared withered faded cardboard cut-out houses pipe-cleaner figures grass verges with their mud weeds dog shit cut from crepe paper roads of flaking grey paint the sky a streak of blue here daub of white there dried up crinkled two-dimension forgotten blur.

What is a child for? What are mothers and fathers for? Eat sleep keep warm environment seasons customs rituals birthdays christmas easter holidays no building blocks of experience dickens bleak all the same passed for another child state school ink monitors books pupils teachers if not inspiration cars families pass by a wave from a carefree face catches sight of a kindred spirit not the husk spinning out fourth fifth hour in a wet bus shelter. Summers came went people took buses to the seaside buckets spades picnics christmases with their peculiar urgent activity about nothing child walks the streets anyone noticed? Are dead children an embarrassment? Broken leg TB might have got him attention but also reassurance he'd soon be back to his old self. What would have happened had his teacher noticed something? A meeting?

> *"Well, it's difficult to explain … he is rather odd, strange … doesn't seem to be … he's here but not here, really, almost like he has a mental handicap."*

17

"Does he have one do you think, is he inattentive, distracted … doesn't apply himself?"

"No … I'm not sure, I don't think he has a mental handicap, nor is it misbehaviour. There's no indiscipline. He even seems to be bright in some ways; it's more that he is distracted, withdrawn, unhappy … can't concentrate or focus … he isn't there really. There's something lost and unpleasant about him … a bit dirty and neglected, smelly. He may come from a very poor home. I am rather concerned about him."

"I hear what you say, but I'm not sure we can call in social services each time we have a child who is unhappy and gives off an unpleasant smell …

[laughter]

… we don't have evidence of anything to warrant intervention, do we? Has he done anything wrong since he's been here? Have his parents told us he is a problem?"

"No, nothing wrong. I haven't met his parents so I don't have any evidence of problems at home. There have been quite a few missed days since he started, so there is some truancy …"

"It sounds like he's a child who is finding it difficult to mix. It's still early days and it takes time for some of them to fit in. There are quite a few like him this year … take that boy Bailey in Class 2 who hasn't settled and who never seems to say a word except, I'm told, for the occasional obscenity and who smells to high heaven … we've had to be in touch with the parents I can tell you …"

[laughter]

"… I think we should give this one a note to take home about the truancy. The parents must be aware of it and

18

when they learn that we know their five-year-old is truanting it will get their attention. Meanwhile, unless he becomes disruptive or his work or the truanting worsens, I think we should wait and see how things go, don't you?

"Anything else? No … right … lunch!"

No such meeting who can blame them? You can't look into every case of   unhappiness   can you? It can't be a school's fault if parents fail to inform them their child has problems can it? The trouble is truancy uncommon so young not unheard of nip it in the bud responsible liberal thinking we expect of our state schools wouldn't you say?

Eyes twitched not a squint exactly darted left right right left faster than darting if eyes could rattle his would have lack of control embarrassed him kept his head at forty-five degrees up and down avoid eye contact people might notice down near people up when alone twitching stopped made the connection isolation solved the problem again except for alone too long difficult to breathe thought wheezing normal body-persons did it slow down inert barely breathing pains tiredness cuts lice in hair washed out in pond water splinters boils scabs writhing carbuncle almost put him in hospital day night wound could not be touched under no circumstances.

Difficulties multiplied like hyenas circling a camp an obstacle like the grey box requires a solution getout-stayout return only when unavoidable under cover of darkness. Hunger a problem with a solution eatasmu-chasyoucannow parents hunger teachers reading writing silence rules punishments lice incontinence wheezing headaches rattling eyes carbuncles keep track impossible Four Principles blunt instruments against Hannibal ink monitors writing body-persons nothing new bend

19

Principles to fit don't fit. Extension of the withdrawal strategy undetectable (at first to his mother) camouflage in The Woods indistinguishable from barkleavesshadows extended camouflage to hedgesgrassvergeswallsbuildingsair no contact invisible a ghost difficulties overboard one by one anything unwilling to give up? Not difficult to cross off history ink monitoring rules punishments harder to write off break times sometimes hid behind a pillar watch children talk play. Couldn't play wondered what play was small voices cast a spell:

> *"Wanna play tick?"*
> *"Naaah …"*
> *"Come on … hide 'n' seek?"*
> *"Yeah!"*

Off they ran. Where did it come from? Squinting in a dark room knew it was good weren't hurting each other laughing. Sports field took some giving up wasn't good at sport wasn't bad at sport conspicuous occasional pictures in his "mind" run round the field in the breeze warm day outstretched arms fly like a plane cramped chest head pain gave up wouldn't give it up really could be kept in the mind do you hear this?   In   the   mind.   Obstacles stripped of significance distance between him and torment invisibility fears hopes mothballed lifeblood for thinking drained away child awake out cold asleep out cold till seventeen cold sleep interrupted by daymares nightmares intensity that could make him feel he was losing his mind. Do you hear this? Whose idea? Losing his mind? Unaware it was for the best   the   mind   his   mind   in   mind   long   lost.

CHAPTER THREE

Jackinboxghost

Become nothing when nothing turn into a ghost grey box violent school become nothing ghost invisibility takes over better than before nothing happened for years the woman called mother's berserk routines.

"For Christ's sake get out of my SIGHT!"

The man called father's alcohol derision:

"You? YOU? Melodrama … melodramatic bag of wind …"

Terror strikes when and where it likes shame strikes with derision you believe. No mind to settle crusher jerks twitches lapses ghost slows jerks empty scent of nothing no feelings distant sit watch sheet of apathy so thick to petrify all things living. Petrifaction nature's antidote inters you underground camouflaged unlit place no crusher no matter how frenzied reaches treasure (do you hear this?) Buried hiding place no one can find without a map frequently mislaid in tatters missing its owner eventually loses interest no longer worth the trouble. An automaton forgettable pest difficult to deal with disappears melts hobbles towards a senseless end. A few proto   "body-person"   automata take a midlife interest in cartography or psychology find something anything before the end what was the point of it all? One outcome probably the worst of all for automata unwilling to face the truth give up on their abusers stay with them hate them comply with them serve them try to love them change them—do you hear this?—Destroyed by them insanity last option to keep mortal remains delusional ideas intact no treasure no map no unlit hiding place oozing cadavers demanding special handling these are the true lost souls. Scum that drains away. Is it for this degree of ruination that "the last shall come first" was thought up before it was forgotten?

Automaton ghost life primary school buried remaining body-person components. Out of bed walk sit security camera detects movement where actions lead safety otherwise. Silent drifting streets school safe slip into seat unnoticed out of harm's way for a time   time   under these circumstances forever. Low level surveillance blinking camera dot small ancient body still under the woman called mother's outbursts knew he *must* have done it to enrage her this much (born the wrong person) four years brainwracking no difference forced to The Woods give up withdrawal nothing not "relaxing" doing nothing for hours watch limbs nothing upended by wakemares packs of wolves in The Woods panic sprint to the roadside sight of cars. Teacher bully Mr L. Adamson BSc entered classroom cracked black brogues fluorescent glint tap dance for children *he knew he was still in The Woods* unable to suppress giggles *knew* no one could hear him jumped out of booming skin.

"What are YOU laughing at?!"

Shocked caught out then looked through binoculars turned the wrong way round everything far off volume down less threatening no feelings no difference between awake asleep not a psychopath out of commission blurred vision feelings speech conversation useless. Shocked later found people took drugs to get out of their minds couldn't grasp being out of his mind since birth.

Net trawled for thoughts feelings sensations kill fish no seeing hearing speaking anything   *"mentally handicapped, is he?"*   In the gloaming without gloaming mortified except one crazy sudden moment against his will uncontrollable urge to talk couldn't talk didn't want to talk go on talk! mutated a ghost to a jack-in-the-box in out in out spout gibberish nineteen to the dozen like everybody else! no he isn't! yes he is! avoid shame! no matter. Stop! Go! Teacher Miss Rowland said:

> *"Now, boys and girls, do you know what the Blue Riband is?"*[1]

Uninvited demented hare launched speech ships knew it knew it lived near Liverpool heard about ships sea ships come on!

> *"Ssssa prize Miss is you see Miss sssa a a prize the best ship the cleanest ship goes across the Atlantic Ocean*

*Miss cleanest one Miss you know Miss looks best you
see they make it look nice cleaning polishing like Miss
everywhere Miss make it shiny Miss gezza prize Miss a
nice prize Miss know what I mean Miss?"*

Nodded she did

"I see. Thank you."

Changed subject. "Thank you"! Correct! Norranidiot
didn't make it up didn't feel made up glow right she said
so pride. Success brings visibility someone to shout at
him hit him fold twist body in on itself disappear.

Mr C. Dearden BA Scottish man called headmaster
accent ginger wavy hair stood still teetering falling over
spoke at the end of the year.

"Naaaaah then, chellren. Goo morrnen."
"Moooorning, Missster Dearden …"
*"Ye'll aahl know, 'aahm shoor, thet it'll soon be
Chressmess Taime, en aah amajan ye canna wait fer
Fatha Chressmess an' all the presents y'eev assked him
fer. Terday, aah wanna tell ye a wee bit about wha' will be
heppnen ness yeer efter the Chressmess horladee …"*

Couldn't understand a word scanned children Algy boy-
genius cross between a mole and coconut engrossed
nodding snuffling. David quiet clever Brylcreem hair
concentrating Lorna the blonde bombshell couldn't look
at her let alone speak even she listened he was in trouble not understanding a thing again flat spin can't leave
school have to (first choice) winter coming The Woods
too cold can't stay in class (second choice) blanket withdrawal security camera hadn't worked what to do? Last
resort banish everything cut off proto-thoughts launch

into space rid himself of himself what goes up comes down orphans pests fight them off doorstep hordes you can't let in torment you've cast out. Wrong useless to the people called parents parasite sickening demands failed to leave he had to how does a three- or four-year-old leave? Hours? Days? Decision no child can take into oblivion eat stay out strategy he must leave what to do? Her need to rid her of him now his need to rid him of himself eye to eye her opinions his opinions the truth is children *should* love their mothers and fathers shouldn't they? If not blamed cast out some diagnosed mentally ill how many adults think they should love their parents but don't are convinced it is their fault their parents didn't love them?

Age of ten ghost failure unmasked too much school too many people parents bullies emergency plan look like someone look like a pupil all that was left. Listen to what teachers say read homework two three times doesn't matter orphaning skills take out fear of books to The Woods bedroom work by rote memorise no explaining the fact he passed the "Eleven Plus" exam separates brain boxes from duffers "grammar school" success stories "secondary modern schools" deadbeats for a factory or hairdressing salon one drab May morning drifting in like a leaf paper pencil thirty minutes bored toilet wandered off to The Woods free again.

"Congratulations."

A woman called teacher speaking

"You have a place at Wirral Grammar School. There are things you will need to learn. You'll wear a school uniform. It's a school with more pupils than here, 800 this coming year, and you'll be joining a House. A House has

25

*its own name and colour. Your mother and father will
explain all about it when they get a letter from the school.
Isn't it exciting? A real opportunity!"*

Uniform? 800? house? mother? father? *"congratulations"?* More congratulations Algy coconut mole going to posh "Birkenhead School" drifted into thinking he was going with him maybe he could be him the only one he didn't fear bumbling chortly odd didn't go with him didn't be him didn't see him again didn't know what "Wirral Grammar School" was grey box letter tie jacket badge *"Sapientia Janua Vitae"*[2] is this what "congratulations" means? Care? Asking a mistake.

> *"How am I supposed to know? Wear them and just go
> to school."*

Hadn't she bought them? The man called father? The school? Someone finished with them? Badge for someone else. Daily emergencies survival isolation his fare didn't want more changes whatever they were expected nothing from a new school dealing with it a demand he couldn't handle in this if in nothing else he was right.

Notes

1. The Blue Riband, also known as the Hales Trophy, is an award for the ocean liner that makes the fastest crossing of the North Atlantic.
2. "Wisdom is the Gateway to Life".

CHAPTER FOUR

Parentheses

Parents separated he the girl called sister out of school on a bus to the woman called mother's parents' Birkenhead pub nothing said under empty dark roof room of a Victorian building instructed to "behave" not go down into the pub bar relief of a week or two away from the grey box the mother caged animals crept around finally down to the ground floor through urine beer fog-filled dark wood bar littered sawdust cigarette ends sailors Teddy Boys workmen smoked singing drunk asleep. Didn't trust these any surroundings The Woods exception even there winter biting rainstorms no rules expected the worst. Parachuted without explanation dangerous backwater The Woods miles away did what he did in a crisis walked the streets. Pub side door slipped out people called grandparents asleep plod pavements Birkenhead bomb site interesting building appearing accidentally out of a wrong turn into a food market corrugated steel brick outside open air part sold clothes hardware cheap toys uniform lines of trousers tea towels can-openers batteries transistor radios dull except the men who sold things from backs of vans the same sing-song shout performance spat out fast:

> *"Aaaaaaaaaaaaaaaaaaaaaaaammm … nogonnorraska-*
> *pound … Aaaaaaaaaaaaaaamm … nogonnaraskten-*
> *bob … norrevenfivebob … noladies … t'youladies …*
> *speciallyyouluv … norreven'alfacrown … comeonlu-*
> *vamgivinthestuffaway … allaaaaammgonnaraskis …*
> [crescendo: claps thumps table or side of van] *two-*
> *bobthelot! … thassitluv … twobob … thereyerareluv …*
> *anyouluv?"*

Build-up swerved before the climax threat of the man losing money giving stuff away had to sell at this price the tone defeat brimmed with pain anger don't steal food the mouths of children no money stole away avoided outdoor market. Indoor food market different scrum of big women men in white coats painted lit-up signs stalls everything to eat corned beef chickens fish cheese bread cakes vegetables anonymous in the throng tacked up and down the aisles gaped stacks of food drink in hubbub aromas wafting into each other invisible entertainment people crowd round a stall nibbling bits of cheese steal-ing? He got it the man put out bowls of cut-up cheese to sample no money the man busy with customers sidled by grabbed a handful of "lancashire" cheese melted into the dense crowd no need to run bodies coats bags prams camouflaged mouth exploded taste invisible *and* food mind exploded nothing like luscious white crumbly creamy damp with shivery tang stuff meal drink sweet all in one or two hours alive mouth body tingle lights chatter drift aisles close enough to people to touch red peppers rabbits pigs' heads raspberries green things he'd never seen. Visit each week busiest time wait for his moment complimentary handful once or twice a fallen grape or plum collected odd pennies around the pub bomb site enough for a quarter pound wedge of lancashire cheese eat in one sashaying trip down the aisles with the change bought a banana the effect as transporting not quite such a high class problem not why cheese and bananas tasted good why they tasted so *different*. This was the life. Walk back from the market on a banana cheese day a dark figure marching up the hill trilby glinting overalls swished stopped embarrassment stared at each other speechless the man called father broke the silence fished a two shilling piece from the pocket of the overalls.

"*Here,*" he said.

Two shillings.   A   lot   of   money.   At a loss for words the woman called mother ordered him to have nothing to do with the man called father open mouth nothing came out it said.

"*I … I can't …*"

Defeat rippled across the man called father's face curled lip of contempt he knew.

"*Right!*" he rasped,

Shoving the coin back stalked off unable to get away fast enough the child called son horribly wrong hadn't cared about the money too much did know he was in trouble with both of them week later move to a tiny terraced house in back menai street by birkenhead docks safe house prevent the man called father from getting at them? Room downstairs back kitchen coal bunker outside toilet room upstairs no blade of grass people dirty angry looks the truth was neither he nor his sister harmed by any of them only by the people called the mother and father. Move another strange place too much think only of what next knew was bad didn't know what did what he did under siege walked streets sleepwalked waking dreams if he was lucky after enough walking he felt nothing.

One more unexpected good thing happened after the cheese route to the Food Hall from the safe house for the sake of it turned into wide Conway Street tracks stopped rooted to the spot couldn't take it in ten minutes or more in front of "Palace Motors" run-down used car dealer a new pink American convertible chrome white plastic interior three four times the size of a normal car breathtakingly enormously beautiful. Padded tiptoe soundless unhinged to not dematerialise swooping fins off the back topped by red blackpool lights chrome strips boot the size of a football pitch bumpers from a ship roof down inside white sofas! Steering wheel white! Rapt round bodywork millions of metal flecks colour of candy floss wheels giant olympic medals door handles the size of his arm magic words—*"pontiac catalina"*—dashed off silver across the back.

"Ponn … tee … ack … Cat … aaaleeenaa".

Never forget these words. Don't dare touch exotic transport him to Mars look look again engrave on the "mind" a vision of how things could be evidence of another world the people called mother and father knew nothing about people who create amazing things the Pontiac said "Look at me!" didn't hide itself away The Woods the Food Hall

Lancashire cheese bananas now this were these evidence there were good things in the world? Knew nothing of them maybe they existed according to someone. The Pontiac re-materialised a few times before disappearing back to Mars somebody bought it? Who buys a Pontiac Catalina? Genius? Millionaire? Couldn't grasp something so beautiful in a concrete backwater. Where had it gone? It *was* there he had seen it with his own eyes who dreams up something like this deserves respect no matter what anyone says. Before the final Pontiac sighting run-down primary school in Cole Street side street off Conway Street not far from Palace Motors had to go there from now on to school? To live? Die? Too many railings the sound of a 9am whistle blew a yard of rag-bag children into pale green half-tiled dirty hospital buildings pointed in the direction of a classroom forty children all the children in the world shouting banging desk lids couldn't breathe teacher SILENCED them began to talk couldn't hear head buzzed body trembled stared at green tiles pattern on the wall battered window frames hands shaking under desk hammering heart give him away right hand rose asked in a calm voice not his if he could go to the toilet teacher nodded talking again outside body measured steps door silent quickening down the corridor heart thumping so hard it hurt schoolyard exit burst into a frenzied sprint flat out through gates across wide Conway Street no thought for traffic along a crowded pavement weaving at a speed never run in his life. A round woman with bags of food stepped out of a shop doorway smashed into her white sliced bread biscuits flew everywhere fell over running spinning over and over croaked "Sorry" raced on no thought of where except away for two days did not leave the back corner of the back room of the   safe   house back menai street mute couldn't move they could try to kill him he wouldn't budge. Never that school again.

31

Parents got back together he the girl called sister bus back to the grey box nothing said. Told they were going on holiday Llandudno North Wales. Food Hall Lancashire cheese Pontiac now this was a holiday a good thing? On holiday day made his way to the bus stop hours before the bus at the spot by a bend where hundreds thousands of hours of his life took down car registration numbers night after night for years learning what he had lost. Wanted to be in the cars be the cars not correct to say he learned about what he had lost knew nothing of loss never had anything to lose. No interest in families flew by didn't want to be them saw himself carried along by car movement part of the movement no effort to move what "body-persons" mean by enjoyment? Twinkle of dashboard lights everything taken care of locomotion a medicine in a bus or car felt alive settled on the already warm kerb biding time fresh notebook page something interesting goes by a Humber Hawk scuds past not much else Fords Vauxhalls lorries vans anything moving under its own steam better than him the woman called mother round the bend the man called father the girl called sister sputtering green single decker sat up front near the driver watch learn gear change position head eyes mirror double declutch. Cars overtake the bus at this height look down into complicated dashboards new angles noisy sensation of progress as the bus trundled imperiously down the dual carriageway made him feel something interesting was happening in the passing trees and fields the journey unfolding stared more intently forgot the driver searching for something not knowing what could not take eyes off small copses puncturing the sliding landscape a mystery until this sentence was written. He missed The Woods. No woods in Birkenau hadn't seen The Woods in a long time the journey took him further away. Where were they?

Days hours later bad tempered arrival Llandudno bus station boarding house painted wood floors formica tables plastic tomato-shaped bottles of ketchup holiday blank except for a good thing added to his list a red plastic ball made by Bic the size of a real football netted bunch above the door of a souvenir shop bought by the people called parents two and sixpence what about that? Was this care? Grateful thrilledifthis is what holidays were about best of all the "Ping!" on concrete gunshot ricochet loved that noise pumped up hard would it go down lose the ping noise? Checked for pumps didn't have any how had they pumped it up in the first place didn't ask. Whipping wind on Llandudno beach long wide very wild second morning kicked Bic high in the air vertical to horizontal switch snatched bowled ball down the beach onto waves bouncing breakers tossed it this way and that gave chase splashing fun through surf grasped the knobbly plastic skin only for it to skip out of fingers onto the next breaker dive miss a fraction of an inch in front of him! Furious swim fast gap closed both grab arms couldn't swim doggy paddle seemed to work never learned to swim pool freezing too deep bullies frightened truancy. Make a grab got it! Swell plucked it away again taunting cat-and-mouse tactics outwitted him baffled angry looked round for someone on the beach astonished beach seafront shrunk distant tiny toy town drifted out to sea on a rip tide vast deep water couldn't swim glanced at ball bobbed eight ten twelve twenty feet horizon turned back waved no one saw if they did they didn't haul out to sea drown dead go back no ball thought vanished doggy paddle legs thrash battle fuming ebb current panic pulled out to sea again defeat terror propeller movements no stopping no circumstances long after he could not go on scraping knees legs arms pebbles gouged stranded turtle no awareness landed body slumped face in sand sob shake until no longer able to cry stinging eyes peered nowhere in sight ball gone it was him. Short time little time a violation so powerful it would have slain without a second thought. Trickle sensation icy numb legs wet high wind hauled him back up his weak way to the boarding house mother sister watching TV a fight the man called father in a pub parents ended it next day bus back.

CHAPTER FIVE

All very modest dentists must not eat spinach after portions of rhubarb tart

Mr McMorine did not exist until the day he spoke French tall nondescript brushed back black hair glasses suit passed for any businessman teacher prime minister anywhere stringy frayed black gown shiny shoulder stains tattiest in school a thornback ray in the corridor breeze. Mr McMorine mumbled English apologising when he spoke it French a different matter appeared in class took register stood up paced back forth before the blackboard a patrolling raven head down:

> *"Jeunes hommes. Messieurs. Aujourd'hui, nous allons*
> *commencer à apprendre une nouvelle langue—la langue*
> *française."*

Stopped in tracks by the rolling liquid sound. Mr McMorine mumbled English again they were going to learn French everyday words phrases the French use "what is that?" "hello" "how are you?" "where are you going?" "how much is this?" on the blackboard

> *"Qu'est-ce que c'est?"*
> *"Bonjour"*
> *"Comment allez-vous?"*
> *"Où allez vous?"*
> *"Combien est-ce que c'est?"*

Gobbledegook words no hypnotic sounds spoke again there they were flute-like strains concentrating the "mind" memorising music like butterflies escaping. McMorine asked them to write down French phrases for their first homework get used to the next stage individual words in phrases what they meant. Impossible to make a connection between writing and the sound of Mr McMorine's French voice you can't "write" beautiful music "Q-u-e-s-t-c-e-q-u-e" came out "quest kee kew" what was this compared to what fluttered by? Went to his room away from brawling through the walls recall the sounds when the music returned began to write it down.

> *Kes … ker … say … kesskerrrsay … kesskerssay!*

Each sound given the treatment a list of beautiful sounds finally his own collection of butterflies.

> *Kesskersay?*
> *Bonn jewer*

Komm on allay vooh?
Oo allonn nooh?
Komm bee ann esskerssay?

Fair copy under pillow went to sleep relief always relief preferred sleep to anything awake frightened him another interminable threatening day not this one waited in line hand in homework no one could have worked harder. Mr McMorine looked at the homework looked at him looked down looked up.

> *"Mmm … let's have a chat at the end of the lesson, shall we?"*

Didn't seem unhappy trotted off listen to more butterflies flew by quickly Mr McMorine signalled to come over the empty room felt strangely special him and him together French music butterflies hovering. Mr McMorine spoke gently:

> *"I like what you have done, but you don't have to worry about making up the spelling of the words. The French have done this already. They have their own words. The spelling is different from spelling in English. Not only that, they pronounce their words in a way that is different to the way we pronounce English, as you've heard in class."*

[nods]

> *"When we learn French, we learn the sounds of the words, but we also learn a whole new way of spelling and writing that is all their own."*

An eye-opener the French already had their own writing! Relief confusing the homework had been hard the situation probably true Mr McMorine was the French teacher after all.

> *"I will teach you the words. You try to learn the pronunciation and the spelling and, when we look at whole sentences, I'll teach you the grammar to show you how sentences work."*
>
> *"Yes, sir."*

Went away even more interested in the business of French now that it had been invented. Less difficult if all you have to do is learn it! French came naturally maybe the music maybe the butterflies maybe McMorine's interest maybe all three reeled off chunks of prose top marks twice prior to demise at sixteen. Mr McMorine wrote red biro hints praise didn't interfere didn't tick him off didn't order him about it worked proud of French first proud thing in life. Looked forward to butterflies and Mr McMorine's deadpan humour like a man in a suit from *Monty Python's Flying Circus* announced gravely one day.

> *"All very modest dentists must not eat spinach after portions of rhubarb tart."*

Children giggled McMorine serious stark raving mad barmy hoot what was he up to? Less interesting was that some French verbs don't take *"avoir"* in the past tense but *"être". Aller, venir, monter, descendre, mourir, naître, entrer, sortir, arriver, partir, rester, tomber* their initials dreamed up the mad poem his pupil went around for days declaring all that which very modest dentists must not do. Never saw McMorine laugh wasn't unhappy a serious man didn't feel much about him in love with Carragher McMorine shambled Carragher dazzled McMorine's influence lasted Carragher's didn't. McMorine interested him in a subject for its own sake no loyalty obedience helped him to think gave him a small French-English dictionary fitted his pocket didn't know what to do kept it always tried learning German fusspot teacher never satisfied with the ridiculous sentence construction no music quick death. Thought he was interested in geography unaware it was a vehicle to love Carragher maps figures graphs periods tables Cambrian pre-Cambrian implications of rainfall on population growth in the Far East no relationship couldn't ask for help didn't know help tried to earn love be good no trouble shone in Carragher's eyes he thought sucked into opprobrium shamed by work he had to get right couldn't get right   had   to   couldn't   had to   mistake after mistake poor marks dismay lifelong self-criticism wasting his one chance with a man of decency by sixteen spiral decline swift unstoppable exam results wretched decision absurd put him in the "Sixth Form" class pupils for "Advanced Level" passport to university do you hear this? Hopeless period the death of imaginary Carragher tie two most humiliating years at grammar school written off dragged around school building refugee in a compound ignominy public failed spectacle seen to fail criticised for failing bullied cowed crowed at longed to be anywhere else anywhere nowhere he could think of.

CHAPTER SIX

Night fall

One black small hours night awoke screaming not the scream of a nightmare that stops when you realise it's a dream the continuous ear-splitting shriek of someone in agony toothache he'd never known split open the back of one of his front teeth fell out nerve exposed pain indescribable the people called parents did not take to being woken up to silence him something had to be done the woman called mother telephoned the dentist's surgery at the end of the street demanded something be done yes it is past midnight held out the receiver hear the screaming unlit street jacket over pyjamas tongue pressed against the back of front teeth ease throbbing in the aching night air head made a mistake at one point mouth air struck the nerve like an arc of electricity nearly passed out. The woman called mother was with him she did not scream at him. Was this care? She was with him. Didn't feel care watched tense two sources of pain his hers. Reached the dentist's house the woman called mother banged on the door dishevelled dressing gown ill-tempered man let them in bent double fell into hallway chair head held man called dentist ordered him to a room unlike anything he'd seen glaring lights white cabinets white chair festooned with chrome mirrors trays never been to a dentist didn't brush teeth didn't have a toothbrush nor did anyone in the grey box as far as he knew sixteen no idea you don't brush your teeth they rot hygiene not a priority in his "family" weekly fortnightly bath unusual same clothes weeks months a peculiar cleanness did happen when clothes washed the woman called mother didn't wash taken away brought back starched crisp paper bags "The Swan Laundry" clothes sheets towels socks everything came back with smiling Swan Laundry Sid stayed for a long time at school when Sid came or told to leave.

Dentist clamped transparent plastic mask over face panicked fought get out of chair.

"STILL!!"

Froze dizzy sick strength drained from arms legs an explosion nazi stormtroopers full battle gear burst into the room firing machine guns black uniforms stark contrast smashed white lights glass bullets riddled walls ceiling two or three took aim shot red hot tracer fire slow motion pounding into his temple skull splintered blood brain slid down shoulder thick gobbets rounds kept coming shouting.

"Kill him. KILL HIM!".

Chair tipped up head jerk shook out a ball of tissue bandage stuffed into bloodstained mouth pyjamas bloody blood spattered on the man called dentist front of mouth no longer pain hot on fire. Shot in face by nazis? Face still there?

> *"Hold your head back and keep the tissue pushed against where your teeth were."*

Where your teeth were? Felt around with the ball a hole in front of mouth where the nazi called dentist pulled out two front teeth. Shock of storm troopers no grasp of the significance then or for a long time ordeal over get back to bed nazi dentist told the mother he would need a   plate   come back. The hole in face stopped bleeding could see in the mirror gap in teeth enormous strange different face must have been ashamed didn't go to school for weeks in The Woods didn't know he was ashamed didn't know what he felt about anything. Nazi dentist receptionist phoned for him to be brought in for the plate   tight lipped nazi less angry fear of storm troopers cringing no mask no gunfire pointed plastic triangle two fake teeth stuck to sharp end swallowing raw pork chop retched nazi snipped cut filed smaller still filled mouth said nothing wear all the time clean under tap get used to it.

> *"Thank you."*

Do you hear this? Thanking a nazi for his services? Plate forgotten except for mirrors two teeth stuck out the rest different whiter face changed ugly mouth open as little as possible preferred not to talk anyway plate made no difference eat forget didn't see the assault for what it was assaults normal nazi was Hanton with legal right to harm people. Shut down held out for a time an unresponsive

43

body for mother father bullies nazi to work on reduced the length of assaults no response stopped the mother sooner than if she got one didn't need to be retaliation any sign of life kept her going so the invisibility strategy was born didn't work with bullies didn't back off sport fun get a reaction mock taunt hit until the creature dragged out begged to be left alone just the job. Nazi dentist took him by surprise agony pain medical help dentist makes things better no prior shut down no security camera no invisibility no protection no inventing storm troopers   they   were   real.   Nazi gas hadn't put to sleep head echoed splintering teeth cracking open uprooted   *saw*   the storm troopers not a dream of bullets in brain fell out helpless watched himself die. Blamed himself for the psychotic vision of storm troopers if that's what it was no normal person would think this perhaps so but saw in adult life the dentist had behaved like a nazi perverted care into torture with the connivance of the woman called mother open season to finish him off one tooth fell apart why both? Could the storm troopers tracer slow motion bullets be hundreds thousands of assaults made on him by the woman called mother the man called father rats school the unforeseen nazi split him open forced in the gaps faeces self-hatred legacy of handiwork no different when you think about it.

Problems with the plate surfaced a year later before leaving the country a small flat rented away from people called parents for reasons beyond him the man called father contacted him asked could he stay a day or two god knows why had he been kicked out? Fashioned a bed on the floor bought food cooked a meal corn on the cob didn't know you eat the seeds bit into the cob hungry plate cracked split two plastic teeth flew across the room for once the man called father said nothing right hook memory? Humiliating shaming burst banks of fury flooded each cell violent rage:

"This cannot go on. I am NOT putting up with this."

Unprecedented no sweeping under carpet something changed found a dentist organised a bridge to be made five years later when it failed replaced with another at a cost (for him) ten years later when that collapsed found the dentist in London best known for this work operation cantilever new teeth joined to old.

Nazi dentist's perverted care start of year sixteen small hope for the future in the balance last straw nazi extermination grey box school self-hatred finished the feral "grammar school" child failed to love Carragher nothing changed bullying grey box caved in decades before The Four Principles The Woods cars trees birds grass anger kept him alive no obvious crisis no suicide attempt no one left to kill not that it mattered no goodness inside outside no purpose no cynicism requires bile nothing changed outside dishevelled inside nihilism do what you like liked nothing no hedonism requires enthusiasm didn't want pleasure. Methods of survival not dying the way a blind mole sniffs out worms stay away from drugs fights pubs crazy people sane people survival shelter food money think up ways to get it a traveller wanderer odd jobs Manchester London get on a train no big deal cities work money. Meaningless grammar school year ahead body active a man's need to release energy for the sake of it no desire to join in no satisfaction no sexual feelings threw up problems not seen before it turned out he was sick.

CHAPTER SEVEN

Halcyon days

Rugby needs boots teacher said play rugby boots no boots shoes slip another situation couldn't speak about ashamed halfway season photographs hid found at back no feet teacher found boots too big old boots ran around what for? Ways to be violent few unexpected conflicts predictable moves repetitive fouls penalised chase pull them down hard as you like little talk the odd shouting no   words   part not part of a team ran round the same not the same.

Physical exercise out of breath not puffed the way you get after a workout heave bent double gulp in air after short running lag behind others. Pace himself offset worst effects no difference discovered how bad it could be running cross country quarter mile first stop each quarter heave dizzy stop sit lie go on last the only race useless. Years later asthma people called parents smoked grey box fume filled era of no risks the man called father never without a Player's Navy Cut Woodbine Capstan Full Strength cancered to early grave courtesy of the three. The woman called mother continued to smoke the man called husband died of a heart attack do you hear this? Breathlessness sport repeated breathless exertion thousands of times a child overcome tired cold hunger fear the upshot walking the streets out of breath gasping abuse neglect exhaustion. At dawn in America an adult noticed a line of Black workers waiting for a bus slim blonde white woman tracksuit top shorts jogged past iPod music eyes of the queue follow her as one not ogling thinking.

"How can you waste energy like that?"

Energy their only asset tiredness kills illness the road to ruin kills. Unbreathing immobilised force of asthma in his twenties a young asthmatic Scot friend Kerr suffocated next to him. Today asthma talk of children breathing out trauma crippled bodies minds speaking out. School rugby running walking exercise stole precious air walked the streets kill time save life. "Go for a walk" absurd tired out look at uninteresting things slowly for a long time. Walk streets avoid enemies legs move eyes don't twitch body alive not dead free of toxic bargain with the people called parents adult asthma disappeared not the dislike of breathlessness.

Drink massive amounts of water not enough to quench thirst fill to the point of bursting others in shower changed bent over tap guzzle second third fourth colossal draft had to be very cold. Why? Suck up life itself a child drank little   forgot   to drink no thirst couldn't see the point food different hunger pain quick no regular meals inedible. Rugby thirst deprived of water all his life the last he would see came the idea water would keep him alive not harm no matter how much he drank the treatment for diseases of life.

Surreal selection school 1st XV rugby team one weekend hooker away disbelief mad as the Sixth Form farce humoured rattled a sick joke thought him worthy of inclusion the game difficult not breathlessness people came to watch from the touchline threw him a week after the game sabotaged any prospects in rugby a routine practice match despite knowing the rules you could stop them punch them smash their faces no suspicion to reverse the decision to include him. Sports teacher away on the day of the practice match the one who'd picked him to play wasn't there didn't care the bastard. People at the 1st XV game had lined the pitch cheered sons not his parents not worth thinking about never attended anything didn't know where the school was ignored smiling faces little children flasks of tea in boots of cars roars of support unable to close ears.

> "Come ooooooooooonnn, Wirral!"
> "That's the way boys … keep the ball moving."
> "Well tackled, Steve, good job!"

No shutting out the chorus rooting for children bruised him more than anything on the pitch spotlight exposed body pariah orphan public homeless. Winning try minutes before the end went wild pitch opened up ran to changing room torrent of shame collision two mutilating worlds never again.

Mr R. Blackwood MSc gangly old maths teacher refereed the practice match in the absence of the sports teacher assembled two sides. Hadn't exchanged a word with Blackwood in five years rejected by him too duffer couldn't run didn't know the rules got the ball ran down the field clenched fist thump anyone in his way must have looked crazy several boys stepped back someone launched a tackle the punch didn't break a jaw spiral to the ground thrashing angry knot whistle Blackwood hauled him over the coals.

> *"You do NOT use punching or acts of gratuitous violence to stop your opponent when playing rugby."*

Serious foul sent off few heard the ticking off didn't laugh stalked back didn't give a damn glad to finish last game of rugby try to kill his opponents lost on him why do something any boy would know is a disaster? Didn't care? Didn't know? Knew didn't care? Low point licence to behave any way he liked liked nothing save brief tinnitus buzz moment punching hatred he'd fought to conceal forever one last stand a millisecond or two   indicator of   life?   No plans desires malingered in out of rooms edge of lessons no trouble (after the caning) nothing drew him from stagnation except one final summer day dazed interest a passing Vincent Black Shadow motorcycle older shameless boy rode enthusiasm missing sterilised second sighting growled out of school glint of sunlight split the penumbra of apathy to let slip the Vincent's flawless proportions all of a piece each component conceived in concert with the others a vision of a sublime whole brought tears wash him away a tide of sorrow a lament for shame that humbled him to the ground grief. Could not bring him to look at the Vincent's poise dishonour not the truth the absence of goodness in life blinded him to an apparition more hallowed than the Pontiac vision how things could be in the right hands right mind right world. Another boy turned up in a lemon coloured mini parents bought not envy not evolved enough to envy didn't admire the boy like lemon idea of a schoolboy with a new car inconceivable clip from what world? David primary school Brylcreem boy's dad had an Austin car brown leather seats once gave a lift in wonder at luxury. How many cars did these people have a spare one they would give him? Lemon advert pushed him to look for a job car one day not a new mini something cheap the Vincent never crossed his mind.

Found a job helping Len deliver bread by van to villages in the spring Len let him keep sliding doors open down warm lanes smell of fresh bread breeze low van rumble soothing background to songs Len hummed tapping the steering wheel. At the butchers Len showed him a pig carcass on a dark cold stone room floor being cured to make bacon seething with maggots the corpse eased itself sideways in horror a silent heaving motion millimetre by millimetre the combined power of the maggots moved the pig Len said the whole thing dropped in a cask of boiling water maggots fall out bacon for slicing Bob's your uncle. Wanted to believe Len didn't from then on couldn't relax in the van another problem forgot to ask Len to pay him the breeze and bread smell not enough a petrol station not far from the grey box had weekend pump work got to see different cars even bangers interesting came within hair's breadth of disaster Daimler Dart sports car bowled in snappy guy "fill her up" saunters to the toilet two petrol caps tank one round to tank two bigger 30 40 50 gallons admiring the Dart's lines catches sight of the interior filling with petrol leather seats submerged snappy guy saunters back hits roof boss apoplectic how on earth for god's sake jesus christ save himself open doors petrol floods forecourt snappy shoes socks stink screaming at least no one smoking he thought.

"You're fired!"
"Get OUT of here!"

ran off from an enraged voice lay low a day or two pleaded for job back boss relented pay back petrol from wages yes sir no sir three bags full sir. Watched tanks like a hawk made money asked boss sell him one of the old cars taken in part exchange for new ones white Ford Consul £200 if he wanted it. Months saving fiddling couldn't get beyond £175 turned to parents do you hear this? Trying to get a car for a "family" too young to drive told them this they came up with £25. Care? Can you imagine it? Deal with boss service stay on the premises clean spare time mountains of elbow grease unbelievably filthy the people called parents the girl called sister seemed to think it was OK big shot called father slid behind the wheel plebs in back the only ride as it turned out quite something big quiet bit sputtery panorama windows snazzy American steering wheel peppermint Pontiac sofas sensation of movement no effort go anywhere as far as you like not out of breath miracle beyond understanding. Where was anywhere anyway? Geography said the world was big so somewhere at least he knew how to get there—now.

A month the man called father's driving licence removed drunk Consul skidded off road crashed ditch rolled in a field on its roof every body part crumpled front caved in windscreen smashed filthy like before empty beer bottles newspapers white steering wheel bent double horrifying images Consul he'd polished new from a distance this heap of twisted metal wrecked worse than wrecked trashed thrown away hadn't been worth keeping in the first place. Fixed to defiled in no time sick force bigger than him to be avoided never get the people called parents involved not old enough to drive no choice had he? Hanging on to parents a "family"? Blatant violence the man called father as dangerous as the woman called mother see them for who they are something a child cannot do without falling under the bottom.

Trashed Consul school downfall the mother's broadsides the father's shaming ridiculous children she bellowed he mocked barrage a screaming climax the moment he pounced not even defeat a valid experience. No redemption helpless without a capacity to resist no *belief* in a capacity to resist. The man called father's genius knew the vein to inject the poison that ridiculed him up and down a corridor of self-abuse. Only the idea of money did not die now needed two jobs not one.

> *"If I work twice as hard as anyone else, I might be able to live a life like a normal life."*

Two jobs surviving two people called parents not one need food get money leave on a bus train car hitch get a job lie or you're fucked two jobs day night double up people get money from one job. Left the dead Consul garage couldn't go back boys talked about paper rounds christmas post delivering milk a newspaper round took so long no bike pay not worth a candle. Christmas fiasco post pitch black five o'clock letters cards bagged four hour walk lucky ones (parcels) got bikes he walked slow in snow feet quick frozen christmas mail cards pink white blue large small sharp corners cut skin freezing forget money worst walking the streets always to kill time house to excluding house yellow lights christmas trees snubbed each approach. Junk shop battery 45 rpm record player The Beatles' "Long and winding road" keep going on a glistening black morning the temperature so low froze the snow thick and crisp in the way people find beautiful sat on a low stone snow wall so stiff couldn't move soul passing on not another letterbox lay down on warm wall drifting away hair scalp stuck to ice torn shock nearest front door emptied the sack of cards threw sack in the street got the sack didn't pick up pay vow never to walk the streets again.

Carragher scrawled across his final report.

"Without doubt he has wasted entirely these past three years."

Took the verdict to heart confirmed worthless known all along not hurtful the truth. Unfairness of Carragher's act of a stupid man lost for decades at no point did Carragher try to understand what was happening to his diseased pupil punished a trained seal that didn't perform put his interests before the child's not helping him grow part of a teacher's job wrote him off. Was faith in Carragher's "integrity" the need for a father a mother anyone years misplaced wasted on the wrong man woman anyone narrow-minded self-serving intimidating power self-important thrill of power? Power. Self-important power.

Disgraced end to school life nothing left bus conductor lied his age to get adult money to and from bus station £20 left over from garage work too little to buy a car enough for an old motorbike or scooter local newspaper ads leaped off the page *Vespa scooter, 125cc, good runner, £15* nearest call box still for sale next bus thrust money in owner's hands before he saw it wouldn't get it otherwise do you hear this? Possessions food drink clothes toys money scooter not his if they were they weren't stole give them back. You'd think it might make him value the things he did get from money made from work it didn't nothing was his didn't own a thing an owner a   "person" chocolate bars pens burdens never had them anyway someone else's interest in possessions never grew despite overcome by awe at the battered silver Vespa torn plastic leopard-skin seat cover threadbare tyres wheel into street private inspection started soggy handlebar gear change brakes useless worked out to slow it in advance put feet down first. Post office form learner's licence got the hang of it. Pontiac supernatural powers bowled him over Vespa a taste of interstellar travel did it fly! Prisoner on parole in a flash no crash hat laws soar up down road after road village after village wind in hair don't stop within weeks arrived left a hundred places rain shine no difference passing showers refreshing. Anywhere possible enough petrol save for roads that did not lead beyond where he'd been already in his "mind" the world ended in town centres no exits cul-de-sacs return journeys his fear of leaving? Scooter broke down fixed brakes useless single cylinder air cooled four stroke worn kick start roll downhill get going a paranormal miracle of technology. Change oil spark plug expert electrics unreliable packed up connections broke Italian electrics notorious compensated for national failing by not using the lights or horn. No breakdown put the Vespa out of action for long swoops turns then, strangely, he began to   "forget" the scooter for days at a time couldn't believe it was his couldn't feel forgotten about. Tactile wizardry ever-widening distances from the people called parents slowed with fear dragging himself to ride the Vespa in tears using a theory it made him feel better always did. Shifted his attitude by willpower forced a compromise travel without arriving anywhere go everywhere don't stay in new places back on the road in the breeze speed walking the streets invisible flying banshee beguiled him leaning into bends cruising coast roads would have ridden Vespa freedom fighter all day night if he could. Came off one day on a wet bridge worn wood railway sleepers shone like glass something you learn never use back brake first in the wet. Front brake then back brake front brake back brake weight over the rear wheel unstable in the rain a bar of wet soap gripping in the dry. Car in front slowed without thinking stamped the back brake flick upended scooter sideways one direction he skated the other car in front stopped slid past bumper missed head embarrassed soaked stop people peered over steering wheels wanting to help:

> *"That was a turn up for the book, mate, are you OK?"*
> *"Are you alright? Shall we call an ambulance?"*

Paid no attention berated stupid exhibition of himself damaged scooter turned out to be a small mark rubbed off starts one kick hatred of his the Vespa's limitations broke down rejected for days lost interest weeks abandoned never existed no logical reason for this is there? But then no logical reason to abandon young children is there? Show trial of a later motorbike broke down in car park pieces tried to fix couldn't walked away never to return or cross his mind for decades before returning to the area drinker in pub sneered.

> *"I remember you. You're the bugger who left that BSA Gold Star on the bloody pavement and pissed off. Jesus Christ …"*

Drawn to something to abandon it first car two three more mysterious knocks back axles engines *he said* not so said mechanics pain misunderstood lost patience had begun to enjoy them there had to be something wrong couldn't they see? Couldn't see knocks flaws never fixed every part wrong possessions wrong pests millstones better off without the past in the present. Young man's dreams forgot a motorbike car flat furniture suitcase clothes meeting trip appointment walk run race find salvage loss in the end relief everything lost nothing needed anyway overwhelmed brought himself up angry young man defeated unaware anger a sign of life. Later in life took possessions seriously no acquisitiveness simple well-made things scant interest if they came his way some things did matter books for working man's college Advanced Level exams   "writing"   four attempts at university fifth skin of teeth bought a fountain pen organ tool grafted onto body. Two three paintings not knowing they were heirlooms flea market lamp on his desk leather belt old man at Clignancourt said:

> *"It'll last you your whole life, my friend."*

Kept his promise. With own children came a retired friend's Mercedes car no knocks difficult to replace a friend remarked.

> *"People with Mercedes cars sell them because they get bored."*

Not bored boredom a luxury unavailable until late in life replacing the Mercedes meant looking at her looking at him couldn't do it put off the deed until she packed up didn't by and by his children put its number plate on walls talk of replacing it howls of protest gave up yes they have it still. One benefit of possessions you keep is you get to know them Mercedes told him enough of her strengths (many) weaknesses (few) to stay in shape as long as he can listening to his upset loneliness fear resentment contentment like friends the trees admiration of her surprised him and others.

> *"It's just a tin box."*

The tactful friend who predicted boredom.

"Alright but it's a tin box that's looked after me, shepherded the kids to a thousand experiences, made family holidays possible, handled emergencies, given at least one of them an interest in how things work and hasn't complained. Don't you think that's worth something?"

Blank.

Is it so difficult?

CHAPTER EIGHT

Social conscience

Seventeen unnoticed final grammar school report damning Carragher washed hands of him the sooner he leave the better agreed. No French class since absurd "The Sixth Form" decision gliding thornback ray spotted him in a corridor one morning unassuming shambles a brief word?

> *"So, what are you going to do when you leave?"*
> *"Dunno, sir."*

Bus conducting came to mind didn't mention it or the "milk round" banks businesses army selling themselves to "potential undergraduates" steered clear didn't say he thought it a fair for posh kids.

"There is a possibility, if you are interested," he continued, *"that you could work as an assistant teacher of English in a 'petit séminaire' school in Coutançes, Northern France—Normandy. I have a colleague there, M. Bernard Aubert, who is looking for someone to help teach English to younger children, seven or eight years of age, from the autumn. Do you think you might be interested in doing something like this?"*

"OK," replied his mouth.

"All right," Mr McMorine continued. *"I'll look into it and keep you informed."*

Didn't think about Mr McMorine trying to get cheap labour for his friend years later sadness gratitude a quiet forgettable man intervened to change the course of his life interposing himself final moments at school a resistance worker spirited him away under cover of darkness grey box undiminished violence school rotten unequal culture not for one moment did he think it might have been Mr McMorine's intention or for decades following. Was it luck or instinct he didn't blow the opportunity? Had McMorine identified something? Interest in French? A boy gone under the bottom? To step in a remarkable act in later life read Borges on his father that he was an intelligent man like all intelligent men he was kind. McMorine must have been an intelligent man, mustn't he? Carragher wrote him off not meeting his standards McMorine put   him   first unable to recognise goodness give thanks nobody had done this before forgot about him until the sun shone late in the day McMorine improved his life more than anyone a single radical intervention ingratitude absolved callous indifference wasn't ignorance of McMorine's kindness total lack of familiarity with generosity. Stroke of genius made his pupil believe going to France was his idea contact information the rest up to him. Mr McMorine died his pupil's fifth university attempt he never knew him tried to trace thank him he was dead cousin old man little information confirmed what he knew quiet unassuming a family wife two children comforted him.

Corridor talk of France knee jerk agreement forgotten money left school bus company lied taken on hat ticket machine enamel badge "Public Service Vehicle Conductor" number CC6143826 "mate" Teddy Boy Roy drove buses past year quit petrol tanker driver job a scandal. First canteen mug of tea Roy talked of army service great scam corner of mouth let slip high up manager did deals bent garage owners tanker loads of petrol half price for cash.

> "The oil company manager kept most of the dosh for himself but gave me a £100 bung for each drop—a bleedin' fortune! I was gettin' £10 a week basic, so think about it. One of the drops was that garage you said you worked at, right crook that bugger was, and the way they worked it was to get me to come in before the first shift in the morning turn off the valve from the storage tank to the tanker and fill her up. After the tanker was full we'd turn the valve back on again, and it would be as though nothing had happened. Bob's your uncle! I'd deliver the fuel, pick up the brown paper bag, get back before signing on for the shift. Sometimes we did two or three drops a week. I made a shed load of dosh I tell you, but that bloody manager, Jesus fuckin' Christ, he made a mint! Bent as a nine bob note, he was, 'im the boss and all! I had so much cash—on top of me wages—I had to stash the stuff in books, under carpets, even under the bloody budgie's cage so me mam wouldn't find it. The first thing I bought was a pianner [Roy loved rock 'n' roll], some furniture for me mam—I told 'er I'd won at the dogs—and drinks

61

for me mates. I've been on holiday to Spain—twice! Barcelona and Ali bloody cante!"

"What happened?" He asked. "Why are you working here?"

"Holy shite you wouldn't believe it. One day the manager takes me to one side like gives me the nod the bloody word had got out. Can ya fuckin' believe that? Don't ask me how it happened but it had and it put the shits up me, I can tell ya. He said we had to put the lid on the whole shebang and deny everything if we were asked about it. He offered me a wad to leave before anything came out if I promised to keep quiet. Guess how much! Five hundred quid!! Well, I took it, didn't I? I wasn't gonna turn that down, was I? You know what? Nobody got caught. Perfect bloody scam! Have y'ever heard of anything so amazin'?"

"No, I haven't," he replied but he had.

Not a hardened criminal working class Birkenhead lad streetwise Roy showed him how to manipulate a ticket machine ticket comes out no record keep all or part of the fare "real" tickets to two out of three passengers getting caught scared him up your eight to nine or ten pounds if you do it. Roy often worked two eight hour shifts "doubles" not married liked work money second shift time-and-a-half double time on Sundays copied Roy up yer money eighteen twenty pounds unheard of means to get away for good the rest in the past. Second hand alarm clock doubles kept him out of the grey box nineteen of twenty-four hours 4.15 am start up 3.30 am before the alarm oil refinery workers packed men donkey jackets thick plumes of smoke hated freezing mornings frosted windows shut relieved dawn broke journey over open windows sped away greasy spoon breakfast stand-ard service children school women shops pensioners day trips nine-to-five office men. Roy told stories of escapades in the army tricks drove round roundabouts twice three times to watch passengers' faces was the beginning. Didn't stick his arm out of the window to turn right took shoes socks off rolled up trousers poked out leg wiggled toes to passing motorists party piece rubber gorilla mask back of head peaked cap turned wrong way round pedal to the metal full bus flick up blind between driver passengers children scream old ladies shriek men smile go back to their newspapers.

Driving a bus sits you down all day conducting runs you up down stairs all day sixteen hour day no rest eleven eleven thirty bed haemorrhoids in six months never to be recommended stay seated kill pain don't take money give tickets old ladies children free many offer to pay bemused grateful. You might think the grey box would have taught him something about social justice but generosity was self-interest pain relief. Social conscience kick-started one afternoon an old lady struggled to pick fare from an empty purse told not to worry to his surprise tears came to her eyes.

"God bless you, son. Thank you."

She said quietly composing herself embarrassed him looked at her coat threadbare dirty plastic bag tired face lined all directions deadness in him moved before only by a beautiful car poor glad to hold on to few pence didn't fawn demean herself no airs graces. Offered cash from the ticket machine declined felt he had offended her criticised himself expecting her to show gratitude spoiled hadn't spoiled anything blamed himself as always the old lady changed something. Interest in characters personalities of passengers monolithic view of human nature governed by self-interest people exploit humiliate the modest old lady proved him wrong he'd shown kindness he didn't

63

know she'd shown love he didn't know she got on a few times during months on buses smiled softly awkward embarrassment wanted dignity like hers never charged her never harm her. There was nothing wrong with her.

Passengers saw him as a piece of furniture used to being ignored bus conductor an invisible job passengers not interested in him children make noise women talk men silent. Middle class minority dress code airs graces more airs more attention to clothes vice-versa no eye contact hold out fare gloved hand disposing of rats' droppings found on seat absurd to be treated like garbage contempt not new they did not know who he was it can't be his fault can it? Genuine toffs friendly few far between on buses fake posh brigade experiment grave apologies no notes or silver change at the moment only pennies (large old heavy pennies) filled gloved hands mounds of copper dismay priceless too civilised to say relieved of the weight pain of haemorrhoids one very important man desperate to be a toff drove Roy and him nuts each night at 6.05pm suit macintosh same seat umbrella gloves on seatback sniff open freshly ironed newspaper fare held out correct rats' droppings one shilling six pence read headlines. Droppings disposed of palm rotated clockwise for freshly laundered ticket read headlines. One evening backside hurt no grasp of why hatched a plan to tell VIP fare had gone up pay up or get off bus refusal to pay three bells (three for emergencies two for go one to stop) pull over Roy wanders up two of them investigate the trouble VIP invited to pay or leave passengers to consider. Full bus pull away before long the moment arrived outstretched rats' droppings hovered coughed.

> *"I am sorry sir but the fare has gone up. It is now four pounds nineteen and three."*

Brought the news as a waiter informs a customer the fish is off. VIP pig eyes widen.

> *"What!? [splutter] What are you talking about? I get this bus every day have done for years. Since last April the fare has been one shilling and sixpence—here!"*

Poking rats' droppings movements.

> *"It is now four pounds nineteen shillings and three pence, sir."*

Face straight Mr McMorine came to mind.

> *"What one earth are you talking about, man!? This is ridiculous. Absolutely ridiculous. The fare is one and six. It has been for almost the past year. I know that. You know that. Anyone will tell you. Don't be an ass, man. I have never heard such nonsense in my life. Take my fare immediately and stop behaving like a fool."*
>
> *"Sorry, sir, but if you aren't able to pay the fare I will have no choice but to ask you to get off the bus."*
>
> *"What?! How DARE you!!"*

VIP hairline purple.

> *"I will not be treated like this. Who do you think you are?! It is one and six and that is IT!"*

More rats' droppings movements three bells pull over Roy ambles up passengers mumble whisper.

> *"'Allo, 'allo, 'allo, what's all this then?"*

Friendly policeman voice account of disobedience just loud enough for passengers to hear VIP cauldron of rage appealed to Roy your man off his head report him for daylight robbery put him straight immediately correct fare one and six nonsense stop leave in peace.

> *"Well, sir."*

Conciliatory policeman strokes chin.

> *"I'm afraid he is the conductor, not me, and if he says that that's the fare then that is the fare and that is that. I'm just the driver, see. If you can't pay, you will have to get off the bus, these are the rules. I could drop you at the next stop, if you like."*

Important cargo could not believe ears dumbstruck split second register defeat outnumbered grabbed belongings storm down stairs stamp off bus cartoon guards follow indignant pavement tirade passengers absorbed unexpected sitcom.

> *"I am warning you both. I don't think you realise who I am. I will go straight to the authorities, to the police if necessary, to report you both and have you charged with harassment and extortion. I will have you brought to book, sacked. DO YOU UNDERSTAND ME?"*

Conciliatory policeman salutes.

> *"Loud and clear, sir. I can see how difficult this must be for you. Now, if you would kindly allow us and the other passengers to get on with our journey."*

Knew he shouldn't feel proud of the incident or be in stitches as they drove off Mr Important bombasting at the side of the road at the same time worked hard for six months little sleep saved money haemorrhoids worn out sick to death. Another bus would show up before long anyway. Didn't care suspected Roy didn't either no unemployment those days always something else VIP got the brunt couldn't bring himself to feel sorry for him the little old lady worth a hundred of him. Finished shift back to depot Mr Manager's thumbs in waistcoat pockets legs apart bellowed over diesel engines.

"In here, you two."

VIP reported them Mr Manager livid drumming fingers metal desk stared at breezeblock walls didn't we understand what we had done damaged the repootation the bus company upset passengers behaved like common criminals no sense of responsibility duty operating a public service vehicle responsibility duty public behaviour company repootation responsibility. Watching Mr Manager turn into VIP's flunky added to the surreal quality caught the two of them grinning at spluttering bluster jumped to feet no holding back climax *coup de grace* not a moment longer upped sleeves outburst worthy of VIP himself.

"You're FIRED! We don't want the likes of YOU working HERE!"

Lifted off heavy ticket machine full leather coin bag hat dropped them on Mr Manager's desk crash copper coins rolled everywhere turned walked out Roy followed.

"Fuck me," said Roy as they walked across the yard burst out laughing.

Forgot to hand back badge reminder to this day of Roy madcap antics old lady dignity not a pauper for the first a time social conscience haemorrhoids excruciating lack of sleep ill-treatment of Mr Important. Barmy confrontation on buses signalled the end of merseyside life McMorine note came France job information time had come the thing he wanted thought about for years planned forgotten about would never happen had arrived he was leaving for good no idea where he was going but it didn't matter. Anywhere was better than this.

CHAPTER NINE

Worlds apart

M r McMorine occupied himself sifting bits of paper his speech unusually clear and simple:

"I have talked to M. Aubert, and he has agreed for you to start at the seminary this coming academic year. It is called 'Le Petit Séminaire' in Coutançes, which is a small town in the peninsula area of Normandy known as La Manche, south of Cherbourg and north of Granville, if you look on the map. I have the details for you here. You can fly from Eastleigh airport in Southampton and then take a bus, or you can get the ferry to Cherbourg and take a bus or train. I'll give you your travel expenses to get there, which M. Aubert has provided. You'll meet him when you get to the school. A 'petit séminaire' is a

seminary, a school from which some of the pupils go on to train to be priests, but otherwise it is like a normal school as you will see from this leaflet. Your job will be to help teach the younger children—aged between five and eight—how to speak English. M. Aubert will help you and look after you and guide you regarding lessons. You will live at the seminary and all your meals will be taken care of. You will be paid a salary, I think of 110 French francs per month. Is all that clear?"

"Yes, sir."

"Good. Do you have a passport?"

"No."

"Then you will need to get one."

"Yes, sir."

"Do you have any questions?"

"No, sir."

"Fine. Good luck. I'll leave it to you to make the arrangements."

"Yes, sir."

Mr McMorine handed papers three weeks later instructions at dawn passport small bag set off Liverpool Lime Street station Southampton Cherbourg first flight of life relief unknown sights raced past thick fast grey box parents school background disappearing was this freedom? Settled down journey of journeys flying trees unwrapping field after green field picked up whisperings in the carriage.

"She is following you."

"She can get you, you know."

"You've done something wrong."

"You don't think this is going to work, do you?"

The woman called mother had got on the train an incinerator lit on her behalf flared up excitement fuel for criticism as night follows day relief curiosity torched by dread self-hatred had it not always been so? Past allegations so taken root so cultivated HE was responsible for contempt that lashed him.

> *"Bad, wrong. Stupid. Completely stupid. Don't you ever learn? You'll never get away."*

Insinuation emotional force petrol on pyre of propaganda not propaganda the propaganda says a child's mind out of control alienated from itself must capitulate to propaganda face the truth unfit for life no getting away nothing changes. One twist reserved for emergencies an accusation that everything that went wrong with his mother's life which was everything was his fault slid into his mind as the man called father hopped on board to round off her attacks disdain derision diabolical truth. The man called father knew that an attacked child seeks solace no one being there too much to bear the very moment to slice at the knees knew the child thinks the woman called mother's attacks will not be repeated twice in short succession moved in with quieter instrument to open the gates to hell. Two batterings two deaths self-effacing automaton always misinterpreted as shy shame dissolution sought out as an ordinary person seeks comfort. No peace embers respite too much had happened too little had happened asylum somewhere anywhere recuperate France marshal energy fuel for the incinerator forced him to rethink self-hate couldn't go on like this he would die call it "flu" some other symptom lie low until it passes you do when you're ill. Fresh start too ambitious rest recuperate The Woods the cars Vespa France.

Slashed hope slips into fiction non-existent daydream future consigned to the past past consigned to oblivion. The next minute hour only something nothing the luck of a chancer failed shaman. The future needs the past the present needs the past seen from the present in the context of the future. No one to tell him the more he thinks of the future the more the incinerator drags him back to the past in the present. Evading the incinerator's flames he misread as hope the same thing as a fresh start can you imagine? Spiral so out of control without help opposed to kindness consideration a forgery despite consideration that did come his way in France a fact he could do nothing about safety sleep food water thank you no thank you something did happen in France it is true geographical distance sights smells mystifying respect from the *petit séminaire* fashioned a visor a beekeeper's costume for the "mind" to observe forms of life people not on the streets for the first time vigilance receding a fraction a helpless animal stares around after birth afraid not terrified inquisitive not adventurous. Few demands at the *petit séminaire* shelter care food warmth comfort home. A care home. Home care. Who could have predicted a residential home psychiatric gourmet restaurant treatment no doctor could have prescribed? Did McMorine have this in mind?

Rattling incinerator scuffed train compartment smell of cinder smoke adventure now flight frightening additional passengers on board fugitive on the run guards denounce arrest him leaning out of the window distracts him from anguish train from the opposite direction chop his head off should he jump out of the window? Leaning as far out as possible to see what happened take a running flying jump imagined the thud not the death that would follow. A wave of tiredness crept over parts of him fell into a *"da-da-da-DA"* sleep the rhythm of the wheels dreamed he was no longer in the grey box not tonight not the next night not the night after body heavy with fatigue yet strangely lighter how did this happen? Longed to rest writhing against tiredness without warning floated upward higher and higher above everything the sky a bed clouds pillows nothing at all to do. Woke with a start searching for the start of his arms legs size shape was he in the dream where limbs started stopped where air around him started stopped even in this drugged state saw he could stand up sit down go back to sleep start stop no one would notice no one interested a great deal to take in at one sitting. The people called parents did not know this floating feeling turned into exhausted sleep only this time without the dream too tired to dream too much to take in at one sitting.

"Southampton Central. All change!"

Lost dawned on him he could ask directions asked directions noticed a difference as he did it the difference was indifference he did it it was indifferent not afraid this was different the difference was that fear of people was replaced by nothing when he did it indifferent didn't know if the indifferent difference was a good or bad thing. Half hour ride small suburbs scrubby backs of houses washing lines children's bikes light bulbs curtains someone gets up late small airport lounge a shed really plastic chairs same different indifference here indifferent frame of mind a heavily made-up perfumed uniform woman filled the room with thick nausea showed passport booking form same indifference ticket boarding pass eternal wait trooped out to the plane indifference half a dozen others some spoke French like Mr McMorine.

Whatever different indifference it was disappeared before the ancient battered transporter held together by sellotape and string the thought crossed his mind this could be their last experience on earth the racket of ancient pistons firing confirmed it exploded clattered grass runway dotted with rabbits racket like nothing he'd heard every nut and bolt falling out the eery thing no one seemed bothered. Pale woman made the sign of the cross the rest talked away or read as though death was included in the fare. Were they indifferent? Is this how people die? If people don't mind dying do they arrange for it this way so you don't have to be afraid of death with services to shuffle people off mortal coils for a fee? Tortured worn out beast clawed its ear-splitting way into the air breath held falling to pieces split-open luggage seats bits of metal body parts strewn across the landscape ineffectual firemen ambulance drivers stand about not knowing what to do. Small oval windows craned neck downwards sideways speeding up grass concrete receded beneath a mesmerising change in perspective everything shrinking growing at the same time the world turned green tarmac swallowed up cars fields swallowed up strips of biscuit coastline replaced fields of crayon green the world turned blue ships stock still in navy English Channel (*"La Manche"* he remembered) models glued to paper. About to die any second when the plane blew up by this time there was little he could do watched another heavily made-up woman strapped behind the pilot stand up hand round cartons of orange juice peanuts oblivious to the danger presumably trained to smile in the face of the imminent end they faced. Were flights long? Better die sooner than later? Imagined hours of flying quicker maybe minutes got used to blue cardboard sea when a fresh set of coastal biscuits drifted into the oval craning window wider than English ones fields tartan France? Disappointing like England wasn't it France different fewer buildings no suburbs grey boxes pointy towers different shuttered windows miniature castles did the French live in castles? Blob cars stuck to black string lanes tiny horse cart field black & white cattle like felt pressed onto card no sheep. Plane didn't slow down coming into land ground raced by so fast it had to smash into the airport building trees all dead again shattered roar gasp defiant engines shudder stop next to a shed like the one in Eastleigh painted blue. Eery silence down steps startled intact plane gaped pivoting nose upwards disgorging cars like flies off a bullfrog's tongue. Customs inspection indifference feeling again might have been oblivion told short dark driver of the Cherbourg Avranches bus was he African wanted the   Route de Lessay   Coutançes *"s'il vous plait"*   driver baffled fired off "words" not like French scrambled write it.

"Eh, oui ... bien. Entrez!"[1]

Barked the man the speed French people spoke French shocking not a matter of indifference a serious problem nothing like French days of machine gun French took to the radio news catch words like grabbing fish at mackerel speeds incomprehensible never ugly the taste of butter-fly music worth it. The man called father called him false for learning a language airs graces pronunciation wanted something better to come out of his mouth the man called father himself.

Head spinning bus journey to Coutançes.

Rauville-la-Bigot, Quettetôt, Bricquebec, Saint-Sauveur-le-Vicomte, Neuf-Mesnil, La-Hayes-du-Puit, Angoville-sur-Ay, Lessay, Hotôt, Muneville-le-Bingard, Ancteville, Gratôt, La Rousserie, Le Pavement.

Villages towns worlds unto themselves café baker pet-rol pump stalls cheese vegetables meat reminded him of Birkenhead market in cobbled sunshine ducks plod-ded in circles baskets of newborn chicks unloaded from

2CV vans rabbits geese goose size shocking scooter-van filled to the roof with fish swimming in ice vegetables larger fatter more colourful men in Mao overalls berets women knitted shawls swarming trilobites swirling bustling movements echoed ducks and chicks. Years later Breughel painting took him back to the Coutançes tableaux that filled his window pigments noises scenes of an untainted world of conversations so different he couldn't see them as anyone causing trouble on the bus no fear is different from indifference different from the incinerator accusing them dull people no one would talk to him wouldn't understand anything nothing worth anything and so on and on and on but what he saw reminded him of The Woods colours apparitions hubbub on the bus umpteenth stop beyond a place called *Monthuchon* driver called the umpteenth time waited for people to get off one or two animals chickens.

> *"Monsieur, monsieur! Nous y sommes. La Route de Lessay, Coutançes. Il faut descendre ici, monsieur!"*[2]

Driver looking at him in his mirror jumped up embarrassed visible.

> *"Sorry. Pardon. Excusez-moi"*[3]

Franglais apology length of bus out onto the pavement edge of a small town not a village castle wall road sign *"Coutançes centre ville"* roundabout grassy bank children's playground across the road two shops *"Patisserie" "Alimentation"* no idea what why who they were hunger a sandwich with money from conducting a few francs bought at the airport spent nothing on the trip the *petit séminaire* paid. Conversation French hopeless relied on pointing (a) identify (b) memorise what the shopkeeper said she didn't have sandwiches no sandwiches spoke so confidently about sandwiches.

"Je n'ai pas de sandwiches, monsieur"[4]

She knew what sandwiches were food everywhere why no sandwiches what had happened to them? Disappointed pointed to a *baguette* in the *patisserie* Camembert cheese tomatoes in the *alimentation* back to the grassy bank playground what happened next a   thunderbolt   resonated for months years decades changed the course of life on the grassy slope next to the Route de Lessay for the first time discovered   food.   Before food fuel tasted of nothing apple banana piece of cheese the best he got. Warm crisp fluffy fresh baked *baguette* dissolved on the inside crunched on the outside bread didn't taste like this wood box *Camembert* ripe ready to run *"couler"* a word weeks later figured out the woman in the shop had said.

"Désirez-vous   un   fromage   qui   coule,   monsieur, ou pas?"[5]

She pressed the cheeses with two innocent sexual fingers did he want one ready to run or less ripe ignorant polite *"Oui"* fortunately thought he wanted the runny one mouthful of *Camembert baguette* a Lancashire cheese moment to the power of infinity nothing tasted like damp rubbery white sliced mould bread he was used to crusty nutty salty sweet cotton wool outrageous nectar topping warm red berries time stood still entranced. Close eyes melt sun no more thoughts yield to a dream of food fresh every day a sea of plenty. "Pride comes before a Fall" floated across the dream there would be no food again tastes won sank into a sated sleep had he ever felt content before? Years later opened his eyes saw the sun had fallen in the late afternoon sky knew he had stumbled across a different world of unhurried peace had not felt or imagined within him ever. Could not believe this strange countryside quiet chatty people extraordinary food life could only be better unaware it would live in him a prisoner unshackled indifferent was this indifference? Safety? Pleasure? Deep breath asked a passer-by where the *"petit séminaire"* might be

"Mais oui, mais oui."

Old man old enough to know that only interest matters lifted his stick towards the roundabout.

"Juste là bas: continuez sur cinq cent metres à peu près sur cette route là et vous verrez l'école sur votre gauche."[6]
"Merci, monsieur."

The man not understood of course but it was five hundred somethings which was something he would find it. Gratitude was for the food nebula round his body an afterglow he did not know lasts a lifetime.

Notes

1. "Alright … fine … come on board."
2. "Mister … mister! We have arrived. This is the Route de Lessay, Coutances. You get off here."
3. "Sorry. Beg your pardon. Excuse me."
4. "I haven't got any sandwiches, sir."
5. "Would you like a cheese that's beginning to run, sir, or not?"
6. "Yes, yes; just over there. Carry on for about five hundred metres on this road and you'll see the school on your left."

CHAPTER TEN

Nursing home

"Monsieur?"

Black swarthy eyes of a robed salt & pepper bearded pirate answered the knock on the heavy school door.

"Ah, bonjour, bonjour. Entrez."

Pirate took his hand in both of his.

> *"Entrez, entrez. Je m'appelle Père Robine et je suis directeur de l'institut ici, au petit séminaire. Je suis enchanté de faire votre connaissance. Suivez moi. Vous venez d'arriver?"*[1]

What?

Père Robine led him down a wood-panelled corridor a book-lined study chair glass of water awful English apologising in French brought to his senses a reminder that his French was awful no it wasn't yes it was look at what was happening. McMorine said he was good at French how come he couldn't understand a word the bus driver the woman in the shop the old man said now the pirate? The French didn't speak French they spoke rat-a-tat-tat machine gun French not French he would have to learn as well? Should he leave all a mistake before he could Père Robine leaned forward make a point needed to reply at least something concentrated on the soft barrage made out nothing for a moment wondered Père Robine was Spanish or Italian taken the wrong plane wave of anger McMorine put him in this position Père Robine stopped staring awaiting a response not knowing what to say came up with

"Oui. Merci, Père Robine."

Set Père Robine off again another pirate giant turned up to show him to his room handshakes all round weeks of confusion tongues scrutinised what was said would something filter through by osmosis body language lips tone intent field questions avoid shame discovered a device to prompt people to repeat what they said give him time. *"Comment?"*[2] or *"Pardon"*[3] with an English accent meant he hadn't understood English tourist consideration needed scared fool to say more than basic words quiet listen don't bother anyone. Quiet all his life no ill-feeling here acceptance of speaking not speaking all the same an unfurling leaf in the school community of priests slipped inconspicuously into the timetable not responsible for anything. First weeks months met pirates each a personality out and out characters Père Beauquèsne ruddy cheeked giant showed him to his room the day he arrived farmer pantomime taught mathematics no English *"Bonjour"* beaming smile that was that. Quirkiest by a mile Père Quinette Friar Tuck guinea pig snaffled food chattered anyone who would listen high-pitched squeals overcome didn't speak English enjoyed making howlers helped him with French interested in what he was trying to say   what   he   was trying   to   say   confusion pain Père Quinette's owl attention stabbed him under weather didn't push Père Quinette away it was an illness with him always. Not close to any pirate light approach to serious things acceptance more than enough. Language gap not the growing obstacle accepting human contact forced him to swim naked in aquarium of rare species from any angle other than his own safe no one hurt him it was true didn't know it was true felt it didn't feel it.

Parents hunger bullies implicated before understanding the extent of fear of people kind people no control carnage to succumb no knowledge of the executioner himself in a bucolic place began the demarcation of inside outside moderate ways numbed him with fear something terrible happening not happening no sense terror inside *him* not outside him not done to him he could see it couldn't see true not true it was done to him knew it didn't know it was new. Sunny day experiment apple orchard after lunch sit see what happens nothing. Lo and behold it happened nothing happened nothing happened again caused by nobody nothing happened then it happened the fear hit him shout accuse hate nothing happening it was happening. Battle got the better of him for days if proof were needed during an English class children who liked him convinced they were teasing him gripped an *idée fixe* the orchard experiment forgotten barked:

"Fermez vos gueules!"[4]

81

Complete silence odd titter class filed out quietly at the end none of the usual frolics no idea that *"gueule"* is the mouth of a beast animal gravely insulting to a person children keep their filthy disgusting traps shut got back to parents priests taken aside by M. Aubert head of governors asked him gently to be careful surprised ashamed apologised to M. Aubert the class the worst no punishment no rebuke treated respectfully when he had behaved like his mother they were generous lost his bearings the idea he made mistakes about reality depressed him for weeks no escaping the people called parents sickness followed him they knew nothing of Coutançes how could they be there each accusation wrong end of stick humbled vowed to find out how the madness worked. Faith in teaching lost low-key delivery attracted little attention same with everyone who treated him well problems not forced on him he could see that didn't matter. Safety at the *petit séminaire* made him miserable lonely not because of people place the atmosphere laid bare confusion isolation didn't want company yes he did what was company wanting company an idea he could not recall having.

One morning Père Robine called him to his office to explain that Père Denis the English teacher had been taken to hospital for an operation would be on leave for months death crossed his mind was death a good thing bad thing even worse thing relief thing? Would he be willing to help out during this time?

> *"Je suis content que vous ayez travaillé assidûment avec des jeunes enfants et j'ai confiance en vous. Vous pourriez travailler avec des élèves un peu plus agés pendant quelques semaines."*[5]

Pleased with the way he had worked? Teach older children? Did he hear right? A full teacher's salary? 770

francs a month while he did it. Père Robine has the wrong person sat embarrassed silence longing to leave money mystifying

"… ça vous intéresse?"[6]

Père Robine caught a lowered eye

"Pardon … pardon" bring bizarreness to an end
"Ah, oui … oui, merci bien."

What was going on was he humouring Père Robine the other way round? Joke? Seven times pay? Roy? Absurd they were pleased with his work. Work? Shook Père Robine's outstretched hand next thing found himself drifting round town daydream arrangement gulf between his and the school's view something strange going on either they were all mad or he was hadn't understood anything not the first time. Unable to account for good fortune a mini-principle came to his aid

"Good things can happen without me knowing why or for no reason at all."

The last part wrong a sop to a humiliated self caught out by goodness it cut down to size feeling responsible for everything standing in for Père Denis gold mine salary lifted confidence hadn't made it happen pot of gold an old Citröen *2CV* from M. Aubert not before he did something so bizarre put himself into reverse gear.   Called the mother to ask the people called parents if they would help him buy the car. Do you hear this? Action so strange unnecessary had money prehistoric idea that he had parents? Parents who wanted him to succeed know he'd been "promoted"? Parents who wanted to help get their son a car not the other way round? Upend reality again parents decent folk *petit séminaire* crazy pay him promote him who in their right mind would do this? The people called parents redeem themselves true colours this the idea? Afraid to quit hell? Knew a good car would take him anywhere peace brings pain no pain if you have parents even the people called parents better than the pain of peace this the idea? Telephone call took up where they left off demeaned money if he changed treat his mother with respect nothing came of it nothing could have. Why oh why?

Petit seminaire persisted quiet ways got things wrong began to think he could be wrong about a lot about things being wrong a complicated inside outside problem promotion money wasn't a mistake respect wasn't pity they didn't treat him like a child a gate crasher someone with a part to play a role even though beyond him. When not vermin he saw they saw he was a different creature maybe not a person not vermin an owl or deer staring stock still across the valley at the person with the gun before bolting. What he might have become before he laid to rest a snatch of memory of what a boy looked like. They didn't see an owl deer bad creature a person needing walks not walking the streets slow walks to see if he could go for a walk look at people behaviour attitudes *carabiniers* nibbling sugar cubes dipped in *calvados* over breakfast coffee chatting about what? Crimes? Motorbikes? Market trader banter puts up stalls no fights children skip to school dry cleaning lady at sewing machine with a customer she didn't hate the dainty priest floated over the cathedral steps like a young model stopped speak to an old housewife men ride mopeds nod at faces. Check for recriminations mild or sometimes none at all no one hated him except himself enjoying himself enjoying himself strictly speaking a term that should not be used there being no such thing as enjoyment unless you call arms and head twisted out of shape by peace enjoyment. Disdain contempt in his mind difficult to credit until you identify his father at work bolts of flashback lightning hate when he felt better. Repeated inside outside experiment from the inside scraped off a layer of prejudice against people he saw living life no grievances against him didn't interfere left him alone something to behold how people got on. Impossible to learn a hard language like Dutch or Basque someone walks past kicks a ball passes bread talks of a trip complains at government tells a joke is this what humans do when he is not around when he is around? How would he know? Did he influence people when he was around when he wasn't around? How would you know? Experience only of what it felt like bread good kicking a ball like being in a group not a bad feeling not a good one what are trips for? Government means nothing jokes oblige him to laugh talk makes him sick keeping track of what is said next group talk babble drives him mad.

Read Kaspar Hauser needed to learn about humans before he could speak in the novel Kaspar's dream of tribesmen in the desert cautioned by the old blind leader against believing the mirage that mountains meant safety reminds him of his mirage life in the dream the old man tasted the sand pointed them in the direction of safety in the northern city at which point so-called idiot Kaspar says to those listening.

> *"There the story begins. In the city. I do not know the story. Thank you for listening to me. I am tired."*

Closes eyes dies a young man Kaspar felt old eyes close dies from the effort to survive before being able to live. His efforts to survive before being able to reach the starting blocks from a long way behind don't know the direction what they look like befriended people fed ideas experiences inside outside what was happening to him frightening to see he wanted company *and* food the thought of company female company do you hear this? Uninvited predatory women not once imagining a woman interested in him wanted her desires fulfilled against her will isn't this the way? Look nice crazy for power isn't it power they want? Turmoil classical music Welsh male voice choir unheard of pieces played by priests disorient mesmerise swirling visions feel in danger. He had passed for a teenager a few miles from Liverpool Cavern Beatles Derek and The Dominoes The Roadrunners The Big Three boys saw them raved about them too afraid to go others went how? An older teenager on a bus trip Butlin's holiday camp Pwllheli North Wales tasted beer crept onto an empty stage of an empty dance hall tapped on Rory Storm and The Hurricanes' drum kit beetle-crusher drapes teddy boy drummer Ringo Starr strode out from the wings.

"*Eh … you … Fuck Off!!*"

The extent of their relationship. Peace and love. Before leaving grammar school "Love Me Do" boy brought in played on the school gramophone in theory spontaneous fun not an invitation to negligence loss of control forget all he had learned tried to believe wanted to believe others liked it couldn't paralysed idea The Beatles' music didn't have a purpose was what it was too advanced. One or two priests in Coutançes playing classical music lure of intense string pieces moved him inside images vanish reappear billowing folds of sound The Woods sky wind stroking face swallows thunder rain like the lines of a car. A transistor radio in the evening classical music dialled Radio Caroline pop pirate station ship by mistake in the

English Channel (*La Manche*) tinny wallpaper gripping Mississippi blues alternating despair hope not for long classical music put him on hallowed ground he knew nothing textures impressions sensations humiliated him did not humiliate him no concessions privileges liked that in small doses hours days reverberations echoing responses to French food words beside the point where food or music are concerned. Radio Caroline disc jockey letters people want girlfriends boyfriends dash off who he is not what he is ten twenty thirty embarrassing letters a day lonely people women two gays one woman first short-lived girlfriend two years later wants something he couldn't give the idea they want to give him something never entered his mind including when whim mail dried up.

Radical *petit séminaire* food repercussions body mind basted forever not new recipes didn't know what is a recipe fresh ingredients combined morning noon night bread baked twice a day butter cheese churns Camembert leaked from small boxes eggs herb sauces like nothing ever imagined pies flans tarts cakes pommes frites cassoûlets sautéd fish Fridays before since including fancy places taken as an adult. Integrity floored him press drawn by a lumbering cart horse crushed apples from the orchard became barrels of cloudy *cidre brut* with first taste of roast beef (*rôsbif*). Hot crisp *pain* from the oven. People. Two refectories one pupils one staff narrow pine-floored square tables joined up for occasions stretched the length of the wall a locked cabinet of ceremonial *Calvados, Poiré, digestifs* date order to the nineteenth century saints' days other wall cutlery glasses napkins mealtime basket warm *baguettes* sea-salt slab butter bowl creamy breakfast coffee dip bread float butter directionlessly in tiny yellow convoys. Plum damson jam sits heavy waiting. Lunchtime affair three serious courses cider sometimes never got his mind round *hors d'oeuvre*, *quiche*, *salade niçoise*, *soupe à l'oignon*, *pâté en croûte* over in a trice short-changed knew something else would turn up in apple sauce chicken *andouillette* beef casserôle *gigôt d'agneau* mackerel mustard leek sauce *tripes à la mode de Caen. Camembert, Livarot, Pont L'Évêque, tarte Tatin, crème fraiche* apple fritters coffee. God.

most memorable meal not the *petit séminaire* one day driving the new old *2CV* losing track of time place hunger past lunchtime everything shut alarm rally driving nothing to be seen run-down café single plastic table in the middle of nowhere closed peasant woman dark blue white apron at her stove looks at the clock at him:

> *"Alors, si vous pouvez bien attendre quelques minutes,*
> *je vais préparer quelque-chose. J'ai du poulet, ca ira?"*[7]
> *"Oui, bien, madame."*

Warm day plastic table see her in the kitchen see across maize fields not a café a home from the front room food drink to make a living not much by the looks of battered furniture scuffed walls watch the escalope large pan butter garlic cloves fresh cut tarragon blanched beans potatoes *dauphinoise* from heavy iron dish in the oven to a serving dish old plate matched apron chicken beans potatoes local red wine jug of water laid before him smile wisp of hair eyeline speed such skill. Had he died at that moment and met his maker it would have been fine by him. Appetite the weather contrast low expectations what happened who knows the astounding tastes even by *petit séminaire* standards unimaginable as though a cat had sat next to him and spoke English. Ate quietly cries not understanding staring across fields hides appetite lost shame nothing wrong even he could see confusion behind the pain. Little old lady on the bus now this woman prepared homecoming meal for a long lost son favourite meal did not know what love was at that moment love made him sick. No regular meals inedible *petit séminaire* changed all this she gave him her personal best effortless no deference resentment did what she wanted to do too much eats a little more not offend her dessert coffee declined thanks absurd small bill large tip had met two ladies in his life.

Still not accustomed to food when he left Coutançes a necessity he could not forsake rendered an elemental human eating drinking too much ignorance obsessed with a taste (bread butter garlic) at the ends of meals no more would come surprised each time as good as the generous last wave after wave. A child in school baulked at school dinners cutlery sitting with people meals prevented him from getting food disarmed here reappeared invisible stealth regardless of anything he did take life a little more for granted the change wrought by Normandy food would take decades to assimilate he would never again have to starve.

Destined to fail in relationships accepted at *le petit séminaire* no one preyed no excessive demands intrusions grudges unpredictable acts malice derision. Respect not a detested child an equal adult in France more civilised than Britain he came to think so. Despite a conviction it would evaporate any moment he became a bit less tense strange indifference experienced on leaving England a germ of health not secure not entirely dying maybe. When it came to leave France nineteen the first year he felt what a human might be like sadness forsaking *le petit séminaire* beyond him another day made a few acquaintances not friends people he spent time with something not done before seemed sorry to see him go he didn't miss anything more a chill or touch of 'flu. Benign routine of *le petit séminaire* prior to words fed a child caught sight of the meaning of work beyond money speak French 2CV radio few clothes death not around every corner. The legacy of Normandy was food a half-starved half-dead child airlifted to care home waited on three times a day two years rehabilitation the remarkable thing no one talked about it not Mr McMorine not M. Aubert not Père Robine not him. Music tranquillity nature nonplussed him and the incinerator went to the refectory at mealtimes fed and fed well dread melted at sea at sea disorienting less haunting than dread. In disbelief turned up outside mealtimes prove the place wrong it had failed him nothing to offer the idea that there was enough difficult but the experiment never took off. Food no great shakes for average person for him inconceivable don't deserve can't last reminded over and over *baguettes Camembert* cost *centimes* available each day of year always cheaper than cars or houses don't believe it. A child sat at the side of the road taking registration numbers swooped by thousands on the way to somewhere he wanted to go never thought he would no hope now and then he found himself inside cars he admired Citroën *Traction* or *DS* Renault *Alpine* Peugeot *décapo*table plagued by the idea that the earth's oil reserves were about to run out before he'd have a chance to enjoy the 2CV sought out pirate Père Goupil for an opinion the best estimate they would run out long after they were both old, dead men a relief. Threads of a philosophy on how to live not exist woven fine strands of mildness respect dignity ordinary *le quotidien.* Can you conceive of something better?

Notes

1. "Hallo, hallo. Come in, come in. I am Father Robine, the director of the school and the seminary. Delighted to meet you. Follow me. You've just arrived?"

2. "How [is that]?"
3. "Excuse me?"
4. "Shut your foul, disgusting gobs!"
5. "I am pleased with the way you have worked assiduously with the younger children and have confidence that you will be able to work well with the older pupils for several weeks."
6. "Does that interest you?"
7. "Well, if you can wait for a few minutes, I'll prepare you something. I've chicken. Is that OK?"

CHAPTER ELEVEN

End for no end

Would have liked him to stay living working Coutançes didn't appeal rationalised it as wanting to see other places unbeknown trust in seminary growing fondness experienced hate of them an unprecedented advance ignorance of feelings fear of aggression blinding him so time to move on. Leave-taking uneventful calmness generosity *le petit séminaire* staff children making a point of shaking his hand Père Robine thanked him for the work he'd done for the life of him couldn't think what it was the look in Père Robine's eyes pierced him

"Je parle au nom de tous les élèves et professeurs en disant … que … je vous remercie beaucoup pour votre contribution au petit séminaire. Je suis très heureux d'avoir fait votre connaissance, et fière de ce que nous avons fait ensemble."[1]

Undone thanked them an upbeat robot thanking its human host clambered into *2CV* drove off relieved narrowly escaping an unpleasant fate. St Lô Carentan Valognes Cherbourg balmy July day free of confusion windows clipped up movement natural as anything he had ever done preferred the car to people was this blasphemy not a road sign he didn't understand control on car he couldn't operate (not many) shops *crémeries cafés tabacs épiceries marchés* fields tractors landmarks fertile part of France familiar as if home a first home a care home able to miss long after return to drab dirty England. *2CV* battleship grey sailing a well-oiled sewing machine no need for dashboard just steering wheel gear lever pedals check petrol with thick notched bamboo in the tank a car could be dismantled in minutes like Meccano down to skeleton put back together as quickly true invention functionality versatility welded no car matched suspension smooth as a Rolls-Royce long journeys a pleasure cornering above thirty touch and go car leaned so far over people slid off canvas seats upright in a straight line fine. Booked air-lifting fly-eating monster plane middle class people took vehicles across the English Channel in front of the open-mouthed beast Jonah and the Whale. One other car for England that day—a Rolls-Royce! Duckling squatted behind massive bejewelled swan no envy the fact he had a car went perfectly gratified him more than he could have said not for status reasons *it was something that worked* like the Vespa the *2CV* could take him anywhere the limit to freedom his imagination even he could see this.

Nose snap shut propellers clatter angry wheeze blunder runway lifted achingly over beaches dots of little children stuck in the sand crash into them or if the thing did fly his car would fall would out into the sea told by priests not many years earlier American British landing craft all-out assault on nazis D-Day machines bodies on the sea bed pictured *2CV* sinking to join them for some reason the Rolls-Royce didn't fall out.

Flight less interesting sky grey rain English coast expanse of blank cloud heaving transporter flopped onto runway palpitated airport shed final few minutes fitful sleep woke dreaming in French he and a man talking French something about arriving somewhere a bicycle going somewhere else conversation proper French did he understand French? Still in France? Was he French? Not happy all usual problems something had come his way in Coutançes could not be refuted didn't believe it not known before food lighter air unlike the wasteland. All his life own parent body began to relax basic needs met a small space to think baguettes meals sleep work petrol money shoots of music people foundation stone laid by Mr McMorine's pirates scrubby outline of a human not religious no time for organised religion salvage operation in a religious and an educational setting is this what religion is about?

One final question: how many French teachers would take the risk of recommending a troubled teenager with no qualifications and no social skills to work with small children in a foreign school? McMorine didn't have to do this, did he? It was the case that he had some confidence in him to do the job, wasn't it? He must have seen something in him he could not see in himself, mustn't he? Did Mr M think the *petit séminaire* would be a better home for him than the no home he had at all? He was right of course but if this is right it raises the most important question of all. How do you thank someone who has tried to save your life?

Note

1. "I speak on behalf of the pupils and teachers in thanking you very much for the contribution you have made to the school. I am very glad to have met you, and proud of what we have done together."